T0355876

MAKE YOUR NEXT SHOT YOUR BEST SHOT

The Secret to Playing Great Golf

DR. BOB ROTELLA

WITH ROGER SCHIFFMAN

SIMON & SCHUSTER

New York   London   Toronto   Sydney   New Delhi

Simon & Schuster
1230 Avenue of the Americas
New York, NY 10020

First Simon & Schuster hardcover edition September 2021

SIMON & SCHUSTER and colophon are registered
trademarks of Simon & Schuster, Inc.

For information about special discounts for bulk purchases,
please contact Simon & Schuster Special Sales at 1-866-506-1949
or business@simonandschuster.com.

The Simon & Schuster Speakers Bureau can bring authors to
your live event. For more information or to book an event,
contact the Simon & Schuster Speakers Bureau at 1-866-248-3049
or visit our website at www.simonspeakers.com.

Interior design by Kyle Kabel

Manufactured in the United States of America

5   7   9   10   8   6   4

Library of Congress Cataloging-in-Publication has been applied for.

ISBN 978-1-9821-5873-6
ISBN 978-1-9821-5876-7 (ebook)

To Mom and Dad, who loved each other, and who loved all their children equally, and who taught us that everything good in life must be earned, and that we should not expect anything to be given to us. So live your life with passion and be sure to appreciate all that you get, and all those who help you along the way.

Contents

Foreword

by Padraig Harrington

I first met Dr. Bob Rotella in 1998, and since then we have worked together for the better part of twenty years. One of my most telling moments with Bob came immediately after the 2006 US Open at Winged Foot, in Mamaroneck, New York. If I had parred the last three holes, I would have won. And I broke the back on each of those holes by hitting three good tee shots. But I bogeyed the 16th hole, and then I pressed too much on 17th and 18th and made two more bogeys.

So as I'm walking off the 18th green, through the bleachers and up the shale path toward that iconic, grand Tudor clubhouse, there he is, waiting for me in the reserved area. I can guess the meeting we're about to have. But Bob doesn't know the secret I'm about to tell him. I give him a polite nod with no reference to my mindset, good or bad, on the way to taking care of my scorecard. Unfortunately for him, he has to wait that five minutes while I'm doing my card, and I knew he was concerned about me, and I suspected he thought I was devastated, but that was not the case. Now, as Bob always says, I have a choice: I can allow those last three holes to negatively shape the rest of my career, which I have seen happen to other professionals, or I can take away something positive. I had been learning this lesson since I was eighteen years of age, and that day at Winged Foot was an epiphany. You see, a similar occurrence happened to me in the Irish Youths Championship, an important tournament in my homeland. I bogeyed three of the last four holes to lose the tournament. Kids can be harsh, using words such as "choker." I had cried in the carpark afterward, but not because of what they called me. I think the real reason I cried was that I didn't know *why* I had bogeyed three holes at the end. Fortunately, I got over that experience with a solid record for Ireland and three Walker Cup appearances (1991, 1993, 1995) before I turned professional at age twenty-four. But now, in 2006, with the understanding from Bob, I knew exactly what I was experiencing, nearly as if I were standing outside my own body watching it. I now had no doubt at the end of that championship—I told myself, *I know how to get into this position and I know how to win when I'm in this position.*

Until that US Open at Winged Foot, I always felt that for me to win a major I needed other players to help me out by playing poorly. But something incredible happened to me that week, and Bob was instrumental in making that a reality. He got me to that optimum position in my mental game—we had been working diligently on honing this attitude for quite some time.

Whereas up to that point I always *hoped* I could win a major, this time I *knew* that I could have won this major by myself; it was within my grasp. I didn't need to hole a long putt or get a lucky break. Bob had given me the confidence that I needed to fulfill my biggest dreams. Instead of thinking that I messed up, I was thinking that now I had a plan. And if I went through with my plan, and did my processes, it was good enough to win. I'd played just my normal golf that week—nothing spectacular— and I nearly won. I didn't have a great week of holing incredible putts or chipping in. Everything about my performance seemed totally within me. There was nothing extreme in how I played. I did feel mentally that week that I was right there. But physically I was just ordinary. I'd set a plan and a process, and it delivered without my having a miraculous week. I had never had that feeling before. Previously, I always thought I had to do my absolute best to win a major. But suddenly I realized that wasn't the case.

So I come back out of the scorer's tent, and I have the biggest smile ever, I'm sure to Bob's relief. I'm so excited, I'm like a little schoolboy with good news to tell. And I say to Bob, "I know now I can win a major championship." This was a game-changing event for me, and the person I most wanted to share it with was Bob, as if he were my best friend. That's one of the reasons I like working with Bob. I'm always bouncing my ideas off him, and as always with Bob, it is a sharing experience. As much as he's trying to help you, *he's always trying to learn.* We're both getting better together. I learned from Bob that when you're comfortable mentally, good things happen. He knows how to make his players comfortable by helping to give them confidence in their ability. You always perform better when you're a big fish in a small pond, rather than a small fish in a big pond. And that day at Winged Foot, I turned into a big fish.

Of course, I went on to win The Open Championship the next two years (2007 and 2008), as well as the 2008 PGA Championship, all in a span of thirteen months. I went on to have a career that includes thirty-one professional victories worldwide, six Ryder Cup appearances, and becoming the 2020 European Ryder Cup captain (the matches were delayed until 2021 due to COVID-19). I owe much of my success to Dr. Bob Rotella.

Bob has never changed his tune. He has a tremendous amount of experience, and he has worked with the best performers in many different sports and activities, from basketball to football to lacrosse to tennis to equestrian to motor racing, even to music and acting—and of course to golf. There's no fancy stuff in what he tells you. It's simple and straightforward. It's "Do this day in and day out, and you will get better." But there is always the responsibility for *you* to do it. You do it today, but you also have to do it tomorrow, and the next day. And the more you do it, the better you will get. It can be annoyingly simple, and that's what I love about Bob. He's there to help you, but he's not holding your hand. Ultimately, especially in golf, you have to go out there on your own. He is not a crutch. He gives you the tools so you are comfortable out there doing it by yourself. Bob has a down-to-earth quality that makes his approach so appealing. He's not playing tricks.

We can go to many golf courses throughout the world, and we can pick out a couple of players at each club who hit the ball and swing the club as well as half of the players on tour. Yet, some of these guys wouldn't even break 80. So the biggest difference must be mental. Today, so many people in golf love the physical side of the game because that can be measured. We can assess what the swing looks like, we can determine a player's clubhead speed, the angle of attack, and so forth. We are all preconditioned to think that if someone *looks* like an accomplished golfer, he or she *is* an accomplished golfer. If someone is six foot two and has a great swing, well, that person must be a great golfer. Whereas, Bob doesn't care about that. He's only interested in the results. Yes, results can be measured, but how you get to them—the mental side—is all-important. When you are beginning in golf, it's very physical. But once you're a regular player, everything about your game is mental. Whatever stage you're at, whatever you think is holding you back, it's not your swing or your technique, it's the mental side of the game. Today in the age of YouTube and Twitter, you can live in the middle of nowhere, have no face-to-face access to any golf coach, and get enough visual expertise to learn to make a perfect golf swing. The only thing that differentiates players today is the mental game, which is only a mystery because it can't be measured. This is going to happen even more so going forward. The difference in how golfers swing the club is narrowing because of technology. The players who stand out the most will be the ones who are stronger mentally.

Commentators try to tell you that whoever is playing the best golf in the world has the best golf swing. Yet, if you just look at the swings of the top players, they are all so different. Some have classic swings with perfect positions, and others don't. What sets the truly great players apart is their mental approach. A golfer can be playing great, and then two or three years later not be playing so well, and there is much speculation about how the player's swing has changed. But in reality, there is no difference in the golf swing. What is changed is the player's belief, which undermines the player's physical play on the golf course. This might come from a new kid on the block who is getting the spotlight, or from receiving too much information from different sources, or from a physical injury. So what it comes down to is, the only separation at the tour-player level is mental. And that can be true of less accomplished or less experienced players as well.

Bob and I have had long discussions about the most effective mental approach and how it relates to my own game and development. I cherish these interchanges because I'm a golf nerd. Bob's experience comes not just from golf, but from his knowledge of all sports. He expands my knowledge of those sports as well, and he will do the same for the readers of this book.

For me, it's about the parameters of my swing and what I'm capable of. I have won and played some of my best golf while avoiding a certain swing tendency by using a strong and disciplined mental approach and a strategy to play to my strengths and avoid my weaknesses. This is especially true as I get older. That principle is pertinent to the readers of this book. How do I keep improving, seeking perfection in my golf swing, while staying in an optimum mental state? In other words, wanting my cake and eating it, too. I have learned that your physical swing determines the parameters you have to play with on the golf course. For example, if you draw the ball, you aim down the right side of the fairway and curve it back into play. If you can hit the ball 250 yards in the air with your driver, you can aim at a bunker that is 240 yards out and fly the bunker. But whether you actually do these things when playing—execute the shot you want under pressure—is completely determined by your mental game. For example, say I'm on the tee of a dogleg left with a bunker positioned 290 yards out at the corner of the dogleg. I'm capable of hitting a low fade that runs out to 280 yards, and I'm playing with someone who can carry the ball 300 yards off the tee. His choice is to try to hit it 300 yards with a draw. I have no business trying to draw it around the corner over a bunker 290 yards out. If we both execute our shots as planned, he has an advantage. But the beauty about golf is even though he has a physical advantage, he still has to be mentally good *if I am mentally good*. He still has to do his stuff. That's why winning and successful results ultimately come down to the mental state of your game and *doing your stuff*. Yes, practicing the technical helps you improve your shot parameters, *but consistent success only*

comes if you have a strong and dependable mental approach
to play your game.

I often look at the game as two walls—the physical wall
and the mental wall. It can be such an addiction to want to
have your physical wall perfect. But every time you work on
your technique, you damage your mental wall by taking a brick
from it. The golfing world would have you believe you want
both walls perfect and often contends that the physical wall
must be perfect before you can go work on the mental wall. In
reality, you need only an okay physical wall but a solid mental
wall. If you learn anything from this book, make sure you do
not damage your mental wall to improve your physical wall.
If you told me that in three weeks' time my life would be on
the line in a game of golf, I would prepare only with mental
work. I would not try to prepare physically. That's the way I
prepared for those majors I won back in the day. It was a complete physical shutdown of work on technical aspects of my
swing, and it took me three weeks to quiet my mind. That's
where I want to be when I'm playing in a major. It's not easy to
do that, and you might question it. But believe me, it's effective. I have found that the mental game is not a light switch
that you can turn on and off. It takes time to move from the
analytical to the intuitive. That's why before you go out on the
golf course in a competitive round, you should never *practice*
your technique. Only warm up. How could you ever expect to
hit shots right before a round searching for different technical
swing thoughts, then go to the first tee with a quiet mind? It's

almost impossible to do that. Maybe just hit a few balls so you don't fall into an analytical mindset. Simply hit the ball to a target and get a sense of rhythm and feel. Then go *play*.

I learned these mental principles—and many others—from Bob. I read Bob's book *Golf Is Not a Game of Perfect* in 1998, and it was an earth-shattering change for my golf. It helped me to understand where my scores went from good to bad. I immediately traveled to see him. My wife, Caroline, rang up Bob's wife, Darlene, and I spent a couple of days staying in his basement in Virginia. Through the early 2000s, when I began playing more regularly on the PGA Tour, we started working together consistently. Bob taught me how to get the most out of my ability. He taught me that perseverance is an excellent trait. (I had twenty-nine second-place finishes before I won my first major.) He taught me how to believe in myself, to know that my swing was good enough, so I could focus on the mental side. Bob gave me the confidence to accept where I was with my swing so I could just *play* golf.

Some sport psychologists make you dependent on them. That's not true with Bob. Make no mistake, you are independent and in control of your destiny. Bob is a facilitator. He will give you the means to reach your goals, but you have to do the work. This is why his players have won so many majors. He gives them the responsibility. If you want to get the most out of *your* game and *your* abilities, I believe the lessons from Bob in this book will help you do that. But it's *your responsibility*. It's not your wife's, it's not your coach's, it's not your caddie's, it's not your best friend's, it's not Bob's. It's yours! It really is a day-do-day process. That's ultimately the beauty of this great game—it's an individual sport and you are on your own. However, if you follow Dr. Bob's advice, you will be on your way to making your next shot your very best shot. In the truest Irish tradition, I wish you good luck, as it is never a burden to carry a bit of good luck. If you stick to the ideals in this book, you'll find that you will be very lucky indeed!

Preface

Writing books such as this one gives me an unprecedented opportunity to share what I have learned from some of the best players and coaches in the world. It also gives me a chance to communicate what they have learned from me that is proven to work in chasing your golfing potential. I am so pleased to be able to share this information with the many other players and coaches I will never get to meet or work with directly. These principles have been tested and found to be consistently effective, but you must get up and live them every day. To do so takes discipline, patience, and persistence. Golf is a hard game, but that is part of the joy—and the journey. It can make you happy and it can break your heart. It can discourage you and yet it can be extremely rewarding. To get the benefits, you must learn to love that journey. I want to thank all those players who knew that their mind and emotions played a huge role in their ability to perform in competition and were willing to commit to being true believers in attitudes that were simple, understandable, and made logical and common sense. I also want to thank all the athletes and coaches who dared to chase greatness and inspired the generations that followed them, such as Tiger Woods, Greg Norman, Annika Sorenstam, Pat Bradley, Seve Ballesteros, Oscar De La Hoya, Michael Jordan, Bill Russell, LeBron James, Greg Maddux, Tom Brady, Patty Wagstaff, McLain Ward, Rafael Nadal, Serena Williams, Michael Phelps, Simone Biles, Bill Belichick, John Wooden, Bear Bryant, Red Auerbach, Pat Summit, Anson Dorrance, Bob Knight, John Calipari, Geno Auriemma, Nick Saban, and Eddie Robinson. I am indebted to all of you.

Introduction

In the long run, men hit only what they aim at.
Therefore, . . . they had better aim at something high.

—Henry David Thoreau

The ideas behind this book can be encapsulated in seven words: *make your next shot your best shot*. To reach your greatest potential in golf, I want you to set your sights higher than you ever thought possible and to always think positively on your way to achieving your goals. I want you to strive for something incredible. I want you to free up your mind, focus on your process, accept whatever happens, and commit to making your *next best shot* by doing your process over and over until you run out of holes.

It's really that simple, but it's also hard to do.

Playing the best golf of your life is about scoring and getting the ball in the hole, but it's not about adding up your score while you're playing or trying to figure out or predict what you're going to shoot during the round. It's all about accepting your shot wherever you hit it—and going to your next shot and making *that* your best shot. Everything in this book is about getting you into a clear and positive mindset to help you do that. I want the next shot in your mind to become your best shot in reality.

Before each round, I want you to know what you want to do with your mind on every shot for all eighteen holes. And after your round, simply ask yourself, *Did I do what I said I wanted to do?* If you did, that's fantastic. Do it again the next round. If you didn't, then commit to doing it in the next round—for every shot for the entire eighteen holes. The point is, I want you to focus on what you want to do on the shot you are *about* to play, with a clear and committed mind. Wherever that shot goes, accept it and then go to your next shot with the attitude that *it* will be your *best* shot. Commit to doing this on every shot for all eighteen holes, then honor your commitment. Every time you set foot on a golf course, I want you to continually visualize your next great shot. That is, in essence, what playing fantastic golf is all about: knowing what you want to do, then doing it.

No matter how talented you are and no matter how hard you practice, golf will always be a game of mistakes. You can strive for perfection, but you will never attain it because by its very essence and design golf is and always will be a game of slipups. I tried to explain this in my first book, *Golf Is Not a Game of Perfect*. Tiger Woods tried to make that point to the world when he told us he was beating everyone else with his C game. He knew his game wasn't where he wanted it to be, and he could always try to improve it. But in addition to golf being a game of mistakes, it is a game played by human beings who are born flawed and prone to error. You and everyone else will make mistakes, and you must accept this.

When you play golf, you don't play against other people. You play against yourself and the golf course. You have to learn to go to the course with a plan, and to go out and *execute your plan*. To do so, you have to stay cool and calm no matter what happens, avoid panic, and shun the temptation to wander and waver onto some other plan halfway through your round. Everything we do to improve in golf is about increasing predictability—doing the same thing over and over on every shot. Doing this is a key to creating consistency. It requires that your mind and temperament stay on an even keel. Because you are playing against yourself and the golf course, no one else matters. Other players can't tackle you, they can't block your shot, they can't steal your ball, they can't punch you in the nose. In effect, they are irrelevant and immaterial to what *you* are trying to do with *your* game. Your only purpose is to make your next shot your best shot.

As you read this book, it might seem as if I'm hammering you with the same stuff over and over—but this is what successful coaches do in other sports. You have to develop the discipline to stay interested in doing the same potentially boring thing, shot after shot after shot, day after day after day. That's what makes this game hard for smart people. But in coaching, that's what gets results. Everything in this book is going to help you do this. I want you to commit to making your next drive your best drive, your next approach your best approach, your next pitch your best pitch, your next bunker shot your best bunker shot, your next putt your best putt. I want your next practice session to be your best practice session, your next hole your best hole, your next nine your best nine. Make your next round your best round, your next tournament your best tournament, your next month your best month, and your next year your best year. This is your challenge. Let's get started. . . .

CHAPTER I

Dreaming Big

If you don't have a dream, / How you gonna have a
dream come true?

—Oscar Hammerstein,
from the musical *South Pacific*

I have spent more than forty years helping golfers of all levels
of experience and ability become the best they can be. It
doesn't matter if you are a rank beginner, a weekend player, a
college prospect, an amateur champion, a budding tour player,
or even a professional major champion, I know you can achieve
your greatest potential—in fact, I am certain of it. But my confidence in you comes with a caveat. You have to dream as big
as you can possibly imagine. I call it creating your own reality,
and in this book I will show you how to do that. I want you to
become the golfer of your wildest dreams.

The most important thing I have come to understand about
achieving your golfing potential is this: no matter who you are,
you can absolutely reach your full capability—if you put your
mind to it in the right way. You see, the cool thing about the

human spirit is that we are given a free will. You—and you alone—can determine what you want to be and what you want your legacy to be. Your free will is your greatest source of strength and power. Choosing how to think is a crucial decision and a powerful responsibility. It's really up to you and no one else.

In other words, don't let others define you, whether it's another player, or a high school coach who doesn't recognize your potential, or a golf instructor who doesn't believe in you. Take control of your destiny. You must own it. You must believe in yourself no matter what others think. In addition to this, surround yourself with others who believe in what you believe and can see what you can see.

When you are at the end of your golfing career, I want you to be able to say, "I have no regrets. I worked my tail off and had a ball seeing how great I could get at this game I'm in love with. I played with no excuses and no limits. I always strived to make my next shot my best shot." Wouldn't it be a shame if instead you said, "I was trying to get good at golf, but I didn't give it everything I had. I never thought I could be really good, so I never applied myself. I never did what I needed to do to see how good I could get or how far I could go because I convinced myself I didn't have the ability to get really good at this game, even though deep down I would have loved to get really good. I convinced myself that no matter how hard I worked, no matter how much I believed, I would never be able to make much progress. So I never found out what was possible for me as a golfer"? Playing with no excuses, no limits, and no regrets sounds a lot better to me.

In all my years of studying the psychology of performance and the psychology of exceptionalism, I have determined that the bottom line is this: good is the enemy of great. Let me explain what I mean by that statement. You get to decide what is good enough for you. If you determine that for you "good" is sufficient, there is no chance of being great. You alone will ultimately set your dream standard, and you alone also get to set the minimal standard that you can live with, and this decision plays a huge role in how good you will get. It rules your commitment level, your confidence level, and how long you are willing to persist.

Many people who come to me, regardless of their skill level, have given away their childhood dreams for lower, more rational-sounding goals. They think they are being "realistic," but in actuality, they are holding themselves back because they either don't believe in their ability or do not dare to set really high, challenging goals. They are afraid of failure or fear being disappointed. They might not be aware that they are doing so, but they begin to give up on their dreams. It just slowly happens as they get socialized and educated. They might have good intentions, but they are unknowingly shortchanging their careers and limiting how good they will ever get. You create your own reality—and the reality you create for yourself can lead you to the golf of your biggest dreams, or it can lead you to killing your dreams and your ambition.

It's like Tiger Woods's dream of winning major championships. Right before the 2016 US Open at Oakmont, a sportswriter interviewed me. He said, "We're doing a story about Tiger Woods and the unbelievable influence he has had on the game and on all the young players. Because of Tiger, these players are practicing so much more and they're all lifting weights and working out harder than ever."

I looked at him. "I don't know what you're talking about."

"What do you mean?" he asked.

"You know," I said, "during my lifetime Ben Hogan was known as such a prolific practicer, it was unbelievable. And I don't think anyone would say that Tiger Woods's commitment to practicing is higher than Ben Hogan's or for that matter Tom Kite's or Vijay Singh's." My point to this writer was that practicing hard today is no longer an edge. It is a minimal requirement for entry. If you don't practice hard, you're sure to fail to reach your potential.

The writer's chin dropped.

I said, "Well, Gary Player was working out, doing sit-ups, lifting weights, running ten miles every day fifty, sixty years ago, right? Tiger has pretty good-size arms, but if you ever saw pictures of his stomach, he's never been ripped and he doesn't have a built-up chest. He doesn't look muscular, but he does have big arms that he's built up over time. But even before Gary Player there were other golfers like Frank Stranahan who lifted weights. When David Duval was number one in the world, he was ripped. Same with Greg Norman." I was making the point that conditioning and being in shape is no longer an advantage, it's just a minimal requirement.

How Pat Bradley Reset Her Dreams

When I first met Pat Bradley, she had won one time after a decade on tour. When I first started meeting with her, I asked, "What are your dreams?"

She said matter-of-factly, "I want to lead the tour in scoring average [the Vare Trophy], and I want to be Player of the Year, I want to win that." Then without hesitation, she continued, "I want to be leading money winner at least once. I want to win all of the majors at least once, and I want to be in the Hall of Fame."

The LPGA Hall of Fame is the hardest golf hall of fame to get into. At that time, you had to win thirty LPGA tournaments to qualify. I looked at her and started grinning and rubbing my hands together.

She said, "Why are you doing that? You think I can do it?"

"Pat, I have no idea. I'm just so excited that after ten years on tour and one win, you still have those kinds of big dreams and big ideas in your head. I'm really looking forward to spending time with you talking about how to do it."

She ended up winning thirty-one times, including six majors.

Then fast-forward to 1991, when she got inducted in the LPGA Hall of Fame. My wife, Darlene, and I are at the

Ritz-Carlton, Boston for the induction ceremony, and there is Pat greeting some of the guests. "Before you leave, we've got to talk," she said.

I said, "This is your night, Pat, just enjoy it."

She said, "No, we've got to find a new dream. We have to find something *new*, we need a new reason for getting up in the morning."

"I love ya, Pat, that's awesome," I said.

That's what life's about. Our dreams give us a reason for getting up in the morning. Pat threw herself into the Solheim Cup, playing in 1990, 1992, and 1996, and became captain in 2000. She also became active in supporting the Thyroid Foundation (she had overcome Graves' disease earlier in her career).

The writer looked at me and said, "You're ruining my story."

I said that if all these young players on tour were so inspired by and are copying Tiger Woods, how come we've never heard anybody else say they want to break Jack Nicklaus's record for majors, and we've never even heard anybody say they want to win more majors than Tiger? What made Tiger Woods famous was his quest to break Jack Nicklaus's record of eighteen professional major wins, so how could he be so influential? I'm not saying Tiger did not excite young players to play golf, but they did not learn the most important thing that made Tiger Woods Tiger Woods. "First of all, for Tiger," I continued, "Jack Nicklaus was an incredible inspiration. And certainly his record was a source of motivation. And it gave Tiger a quest—to break Jack's record for majors. He has fourteen [it's fifteen now]. We pretty much could have predicted when he said it that Tiger would win somewhere between fourteen and twenty-two majors because we know from psychology that wherever we set our goal, we either achieve it, break it by a bit, or miss it by a bit, but you're going to finish somewhere in a comfort zone around that target goal you set for yourself.

"If you remember in the beginning, some people said breaking Jack's record was impossible, never would happen, couldn't be done. Other people said, 'Oh, God, this is exciting.' As inspiring as it's been, it's also possible that Tiger Woods is a more talented golfer than Jack Nicklaus. And that Nicklaus's record was too low a standard for Tiger to set, and as a result of Jack only winning eighteen, it really held Tiger back."

"What do you mean?" the writer asked.

"Well, if Jack had won thirty-two majors—he did finish second nineteen times—my guess is Tiger would have twenty-six or twenty-eight by now, and it's very possible that Jack's standard really limited Tiger when he set his goal that way."

My point is that setting this standard got Tiger to fifteen and gives him a chance to get to twenty-two, but even if he fails in his quest to catch or surpass Nicklaus, he'll end up the second-greatest major champion winner ever. In other words, we are taught to set goals and to aspire to them. But you need to dream bigger than most people think is possible. To be exceptional and ultimately achieve greatness, you need a vivid and unlimited imagination about how good you can get.

For example, what would Tiger have become if his only goal was to win each major once, and then he decided, "That's enough for me." What if he said, "I've proven I could do it, I'm a huge success, and I've got plenty of money and plenty of trophies. That's enough for me." Or "I've gotten to number one in the world. I'm done." How differently would you see him? How differently would Tiger see himself? But what makes him special as a competitor is that he's still hungry, he's still working and striving. So ask yourself, "What's good enough for me?"

I have been studying the psychology of greatness for a very long time. I am not interested in the kind of psychology most people study in school—you might have taken a class in abnormal psychology in college. Those psychologists or psychiatrists take people who have clinical problems and try to get them to function normally, which would be considered a successful outcome.

I work instead with people who are already above normal function and try to get them to their optimal performance. I'm all about exceptionalism, as opposed to normalcy, mediocrity, or being average. And this usually starts with dreams. Dreams are simply your ideas about you and your life. I tell people that you are born, then you live, then you die. It's what you do when you are alive that matters. Are you going to try to do some fantastic things and have a ball doing it, or are you going to be so worried about looking good in the eyes of other people that you set your goals low so you don't fail or ever look like a failure? When did you start giving away your dreams or giving up on them? When did you start becoming "realistic"? Who taught you this? Are you sure this is what you wanted to learn? When did you start believing dreams of greatness were not possible for you? It happens to many people. For example, some college golf teams determine their outcome before they go to a tournament. They will say, "We can beat this team and that team, but we can't beat that team or this team. I think we'll finish between fourth and seventh. That would be a really good tournament for us." A lot of individual players do the same thing.

Why would you do that? Why would you decide to believe in another team or player that you don't watch practice, that you don't watch play, but just because you've gone online and studied what they've done in the past, you've decided that's the way it's going to be this week or forever? Some people never practice or take lessons or strive to improve because they have convinced themselves they could never improve or shoot lower scores. In this book we will examine the joy of chasing your potential and loving the challenge of seeing how great you can get at golf. It's about setting your sights high and—ultimately—finding out how many of your dreams can come true and how far you can go with your game.

If you want to truly chase your golfing potential by setting high goals, you have to be prepared that others might look at you as crazy or delusional. I only think you're delusional if you're thinking you're going to be successful in your quest without a work ethic, belief, discipline, persistence, or patience. A huge advantage of high goals is where you end up if you get it all, but another big advantage is where you end up if you don't get it all. For example, if you're shooting in the 100s and want to get better, instead of trying to just break 100, aim to shoot 85. If you get it, great. If you fail, you will still be shooting 87, which is a significant improvement. If you're a 12-handicapper who points to being a scratch golfer, you might become a scratch golfer. But if you fail, you could be a 1, 2, or 3. Make it your goal to win six Senior Club Championships and you might win six or seven, but if you fail, you might end up with three or four. Aim to shoot 65 and you've increased the odds that you'll shoot 65, but if you fail, you could shoot 67 or 68. Set your sights to be a Top 5 player in the world and you might end up being one of the top five players, but if you fail, you could be sixth, seventh, or eighth. You get the point.

Ben Hogan once said, "You hear stories about me beating my brains out practicing. But I was enjoying myself. I couldn't wait to get up in the morning so I could hit balls. When I'm hitting the ball where I want, hard and crisply, it's a joy that very few people experience." Like Hogan, I want you to have ideas in your head that motivate you, give you passion, and give you a reason to be excited. When you have something exciting

No Limits...

Being born human gives every young boy and girl in the world a chance to be as good as everyone else. But it also gives them a chance to be better than everyone else in their club, in their city, in their state, in their country, or in the world. It is *their* choice based on how big they're willing to dream and believe, and how willing they are to commit to living a life without limits.

that you're chasing, you can't wait to go to bed at night because you can't wait for the next morning to go practice. As you're falling asleep, you're going over in your head what you'll be working on, and what time you're going to get to the course, and what you're planning to do when you're there. You fall asleep thinking about it. And you wake up in the morning and can't wait to work on it.

Low aspirations lead to just going through the motions when it's time to practice, and even then you only do this when you happen to be in the mood or feel like doing it. It leads to being easily distracted and forgetting what your priorities are. It might lead you to practicing or working on your game, but not to practicing smart or with a purpose. It's like the Cab Calloway lyric "I Ain't Gettin' Nowhere Fast."

We can learn a lot from other sports and their top coaches. All great coaches constantly talk about championships, triumphs, and excellence. No successful leader ever excited a team by chasing mediocrity or talking about it. Effective coaches in other sports understand the importance of having extremely high goals, passion, and commitment to greatness. How would you like it if your golf instructor told you that you could only be decent? Or maybe if you worked hard you could shoot in the 80s or 90s but you could never be any better than that? Would you love that teacher? Would you believe in that teacher? Would you be excited about getting lessons from that teacher? It's bad enough if a coach perceives you this way. Make sure you don't do it to yourself!

The most important quality that made Tiger *Tiger* was his belief in himself. After his automobile accident in early 2021, it remains to be seen if he can make another incredible comeback. While Tiger is certainly a dedicated and highly disciplined athlete, what really separated him from others and made him special was his vision for his career and the dreams and goals he very publicly set for himself. Collin Morikawa, after becoming the only other player to win a major (the PGA championship) and a WGC event before age twenty-five, said after Tiger's accident, "I don't think we say thank you enough, so I want to say thank you to Tiger. Tiger means everything to me." Many players are talented, but in addition to talent, it takes huge ideas, and then honoring and sustaining a commitment to and belief in those ideas. Being incredibly diligent about your work ethic is a given, because all top players—not just Tiger—work hard today. And if anything, as your ideas ferment in your mind, you need to get bigger ideas as you get more experience. That's what keeps you wired. These bigger ideas light your fire and keep it burning bright to provide passion and a reason for getting up every morning. We also know that saying it publicly tends to hold you to it. At least saying it to those who coach you, care about you, and love you and support your dreams.

If you look back in time, for every new generation the challenge for success gets greater, the competitive talent gets better, as players learn from the previous generation, and knowledge gets passed down. So being successful becomes a greater challenge. But maybe for you it's enough to just join a club, to be a decent golfer, or just get to play golf. Maybe it's enough for you to win a club championship or a flight in a member-guest. Maybe it's enough just to get a college scholarship and then coast through your college experience. Maybe it's enough to just get on tour and then coast through a tour career instead of trying to do something incredible. The point is, it becomes easy to give up on big challenges that will push you and make you work and test your insides. In golf, a coach can help you. But if that coach is not there with you every day and all the time you practice, the passion is going to have to come from you.

Golfing dreams are simply your ideas for your life and your golf game. They are things you would love to find out if you can do that will bring great joy, satisfaction, and pride. They are ideas that give you a purpose and set you on a mission. Because as a human being you are blessed from birth with a free will, you get to choose which ideas and dreams you want to follow. You get to create your own reality inside your head. Then you get to live it out in life. Be sure to choose wisely because it's your chance to see how good you can get at golf. Some of it is in your mind. Some of it, as Ben Hogan once said, is in the dirt. And some of it will be in your heart and your soul, your gut and the human spirit.

How to chase your potential and find it is what this book is about. Where you decide to set the bar for yourself will play a primary role not only in how great a player you become, but also in how dedicated you become, how confident you become, how composed and mentally tough you become, how smart you will practice, and whom you will choose to help you in your quest. If you choose to dream big, you'll get up every day with a purpose, you will have a clear vision and a mission, you'll know what matters to you and what your priorities are, which

Remember *Your* Dream

You don't have to have the same dream or quest as Tiger. The dream must be yours, but make it big. Make it grandiose. It must excite your passion and get you up—wired—every day.

will help you avoid all the possible distractions and excuses along the way.

Your attitude must be more about possibilities than probabilities. You cannot be content with playing safe and looking for security, being told you are good and thinking that is good enough. You must be willing to stretch yourself, dig down deep, and strive to take your talent to another level—if you are truly willing to chase your potential and play the golf of your dreams.

It's your choice. Do you want to live your life in what others call a rational, realistic way and think like others? Or do you want to do things that others see as irrational and ridiculous, illogical and unrealistic—and impossible. Often, true genius is choosing to believe in your dreams. Not believing in your dreams could be the dumbest thing you choose to do with your one chance at life. Sometimes you have to dream up ideas in your head that even defy human understanding, unless you want to be like everyone else and never find out what is possible for you during your time on this planet.

When we talk about dreams, is it a dream? Is it an illusion? Is it a delusion? Is it real? Or do you just have a great imagination? All I know is, they are your ideas for your life. Whom are you going to believe, you and your ideas, or some so-called expert who wants to tell you what you cannot do or that you don't have it? It takes a lot of imagination to do things that have never been done before. Perhaps you have admired the way Tiger Woods or Jack Nicklaus or Annika Sorenstam played the game and what they have achieved. The bigger challenge, however, is what are you going to do with *your* life and what are you going to dream up for *you*? To choose your potential requires a brilliant imagination, a joyful search, the love of a quest that will challenge your mind, your body, your guts, and your spirit in every way possible. You must be able to see it in your mind as coming true long before it happens or other people see it.

Muhammad Ali probably said it best: "I am the greatest; I said that even before I knew I was." Ali created his own reality, and you can, too. So let's get started on making your next shot your best shot, pursuing your quest for personal greatness and chasing your potential. . . .

CHAPTER 2

You Are What You Think about Yourself

I can't wait until tomorrow, 'cause I get better looking every day.

—Joe Namath,
from the title of his book

Years ago, the noted basketball coach Jim Larrañaga, who is now the head coach at the University of Miami, asked me to speak to his team at George Mason University. Going into the 2005–6 season, the team had no recruits in the Top 100. While waiting to talk to the team on the campus in Fairfax, Virginia, I'm studying *USA Today*'s preseason polls, and not a single poll has George Mason even listed. When I walk into the room, the players are eager and attentive and ready to soak up any advice I might be able to share. I clear my throat and tell them, "How stupid are these sportswriters! You guys are going to win the National Championship this year, and they don't even have you in the Top Forty." Then I top it off with "How smart is your coach? He's one of the only people in the country who saw how talented you guys are and believed in you."

After I left, Coach Larrañaga called me and said he had had the players write down their goals for the season. He said they all wrote *Win the National Championship* or *Go to the Final Four*. He decided that if they believed it was possible, then he would believe it as well. When the season ended, the Patriots had recorded a team-record 23 regular-season victories, was the only team in history to beat three No. 1 seeds, and ended up going to the Final Four, the first team from the Colonial Athletic Association to accomplish that feat.

How you look at yourself can be a self-fulfilling prophecy. Studies have shown that when teachers set high expectations for certain students and tell them how smart they are, those students often excel and outperform the other students. Psychologists call it the Pygmalion effect. The reverse can also be true. Students who are told they are only average or have no talent often live up to that image as well. It's similar with coaching and even affects the quality of feedback received by a player, as well as the instructional information that is given to a player. The more a coach believes in you, the more qualitative and quantitative feedback you get. Even though some of it might be corrective or critical, it's always followed by instructional feedback if athletes are perceived as more talented.

Basically, you are what you think about yourself, and it doesn't matter if that image comes from other people describing you or if it comes from inside you. The Pygmalion effect is named after the Greek mythological character Pygmalion, a sculptor who supposedly fell in love with one of his sculptures. Books and plays and even movies have been inspired by the idea, the most famous being George Bernard Shaw's 1913 play, *Pygmalion*, and the musical and movie *My Fair Lady*, which are based on the play. The bottom line is, are you going to fall in love with *your* game and *your* talents and *your* skills, or are you going to allow someone else—maybe a teacher or another player—to give you a negative impression about yourself, your ability, your future?

Joe Namath, in the opening quote to this chapter, was partly kidding, but he also knew not to leave room for doubt. Whichever way you choose to think about yourself, it's your choice, it's your option, it's your decision. In today's professional golf environment, tour player Daniel Berger fits that role. After he won the Charles Schwab Challenge, the first tournament without a gallery in the age of COVID-19, he was asked what he looks like with a mask on. He responded without hesitation, "About the same as I do now, gorgeous." You can control how you feel about your game, your career, and your life. Your opinion about your talent and your potential really matters, so pay attention to how you view and think about yourself and your ability.

This means that to shape the way you think of yourself to achieve your dreams, you have to think positive thoughts, and you might even say them out loud to yourself. Speaking out loud allows you to hear how you are thinking, so it hits your heart. Sometimes saying your thoughts out loud, so you can actually hear them, lets you realize how negative you've been about your golf game, or it allows you to appreciate how positive you are about your golf game. I'd like you to say your thoughts out loud, maybe every night before you go to bed, and be sure to keep those thoughts positive. There is nothing wrong with giving yourself a nightly pep talk to reinforce how good you really are.

The Pygmalion effect can culminate in self-fulfilling prophecies. They really do happen, such as with Joe Namath in Super Bowl III, when he predicted—actually guaranteed—that the Jets, against all odds, would beat the Baltimore Colts, even though

Who Controls Your Fate or Destiny?

Is there such a thing as fate or destiny? I believe there is. But the question is, Do you control it or does someone else control it? Either way, one of the great things about the human mind is that you get to make your own destiny that you create yourself, and you are free to believe that you're destined to be great. Then you have to be sure not to screw up your destiny. *Manifest your golfing destiny by believing in yourself and in your dreams.*

the Colts were 18-point favorites. It happened with Tiger Woods, whose father, Earl, told him as a child that he would be bigger than Mahatma Gandhi. And it happened with the miracle US Olympic hockey team, when a group of ragtag college kids and minor leaguers defeated the Soviet team on their way to winning the gold medal in 1980 at Lake Placid, New York. In that case, hockey legend Herb Brooks was coaching a mishmash of nonprofessional players against a Soviet team that consisted of veteran professionals who had beaten a team of NHL all-stars. "We are not good enough to win on talent alone," Brooks said before the Olympic Games started that year. "So we must have belief in what we are doing and we must respect and appreciate what we have." Brooks's team actually lost, 10–3, to the Soviet team in a practice game three days before the Olympics started, but they remained undaunted. In the game that counted—the semifinals of the Olympics—ABC commentator Al Michaels described the final seconds as the US team was about to win the game, 4–3, after they scored two third-period goals: "Do you believe in miracles? Yes!" he screamed. Sheer bedlam erupted on the ice after the US triumph, with chants of "We beat the Russians! We beat the Russians!" *Sports Illustrated* ranked the victory as the greatest sporting achievement of the century, and it has been the subject of two movies and countless books. Two days later, the US team beat Finland for the gold medal. The genius of Coach Brooks was to instill a belief in his players that they could fulfill their potential, and they did. "You can't be common because the common man goes nowhere," Brooks said. "You have to be uncommon." Then he added for emphasis, "I don't want the best players. I want the right players." Brooks wanted those who believed in themselves. He was able to convince his players that they were even better than they were. And they realized their incredible dream.

A similar thing happened with Padraig Harrington in golf. When Harrington won the 2007 British Open after an unheralded junior career and no American college experience, he was the first Irishman to capture the British Open in sixty years. Then he won another British Open and the PGA Championship the following year. Suddenly, a lot of younger players in Ireland believed they could do it as well—the Pygmalion effect—and over the next few years there was an Irish invasion into golf's major championships. Graeme McDowell won the 2010 US Open at Pebble Beach, Rory McIlroy won four majors in a five-year span, Darren Clarke won the 2011 British Open, and Shane Lowry won the 2019 British Open. After Harrington proved that Irish golfers could be world-beaters, these guys started to believe in themselves and their ability. Hideki Matsuyama, after his compelling and historical victory in the 2021 Masters, withstanding the enormous pressure of being the first Asian to win at Augusta, might have a similar effect on the young players of Japan in the years to come.

To make your wildest dreams a reality, you must believe in what you are doing, and you must respect and appreciate what you have, because you take your game, your personality, your mind, your body, and your skills to the course every day. You have to create the kind of magic that Herb Brooks did when he said to his miracle hockey team, "Go shock the world." But if a coach isn't doing it for you, then *you* have to plant seeds in your own head every day.

It's important to forget what other people are saying about you (unless it's positive and supportive) and create your own confidence. When Hal Sutton was playing head-to-head against Tiger Woods in the 2000 Players Championship, Sutton said before the final round, "I am sick of everybody else's thoughts and feelings about me and my game and thinking I'm crazy to think I can beat Tiger and win." Remember, this was the year that Tiger won the US Open at Pebble Beach by fifteen shots, the British Open at St Andrews by eight strokes, and beat Bob May in a playoff at the PGA Championship at Valhalla Golf Club.

As Sutton was watching his 6-iron approach flying toward the flag on the final hole, he famously said, "Be the right club *today*." Later, he explained that he had built up so much emotion inside and it all came out because he was so into the moment. He said he had anticipated before the round that Tiger would eagle 16, and they would have a dogfight on the last two holes. Sutton prepared his mind for that and it paid off, because—sure enough—Woods birdied the 13th hole and eagled the par-5 16th to move within a stroke of Sutton heading to the 17th, with its treacherous island green. Both players parred 17, so they came to the 440-yard, par-4 18th, with water down the entire left side of the fairway and green, and Tiger one shot behind. After his perfect tee shot, Sutton's striped 6-iron covered the flag and finished eight feet from the cup. He beat Tiger on that day, fulfilling his prophecy. When members of the media asked Sutton how he could possibly beat Tiger in a major tournament on a super difficult course such as the TPC, Sutton answered, "Well, last night I got down on my knees to say my prayers before I got in bed, as I always do, and it hit me that I'm not praying to Tiger Woods, so Tiger Woods must not be God."

This is all well and good for certain tour players who have learned to master their mind, but how do *you* get to the point where you are able to create a positive image for *you* and *your* game? First of all, don't be too hard on yourself. You don't have to play perfect. It's always interesting that with your love life or your relationships or someone you're first dating, you would never think of getting them to like you more by constantly picking on them. However, for some reason golfers think the more they pick on their game, the better they are going to get. All that does is cause you to become more sensitive and doubtful about your game and your ability. It's hard to fall in love with yourself on the golf course if you're constantly picking your game apart. You wouldn't do it to someone else, so don't do it to yourself. It's okay to see yourself as not being as physically gifted as other people, but then you must decide that you're going to beat them with your dedication to other parts of the game—your mental toughness, your patience, your resilience, your grit, your staying in the moment, as well as your course management and your short game.

Play for Yourself, Not for Others

Almost all play their best when they're playing for their own standards and expectations. That's more than enough to deal with. Playing for other people's expectations always leads to problems. It's like the musician in the back of the bar who is playing his heart out while most of the patrons are talking to one another, oblivious to the music. Just like that musician, you must learn to play for your personal joy and satisfaction. Even if people give you grief—or praise you— for what you shot, two minutes later they're not thinking about you and your score anymore. They really don't care that much about you.

There are a lot of different kinds of talent, including talent on the inside. To be the best you can be, you don't have to be a physical specimen and bomb it. But you can develop a superior wedge game. Or learn to be more accurate with your approach shots. Or create a better putting stroke and become an excellent putter. All of these will contribute to your self-fulfilling prophecy of being a great golfer. Another of those talents is emotional maturity. That's something you can create yourself, being more together than other players. You can be more persistent. You can create your own mental toughness. During a round, tell yourself to hang in there for the entire eighteen holes. Whatever you do, decide you will not give it away. If you don't have everybody else telling you how good you are, you have to believe in yourself more than other people believe in you. Understand that part of your job is to fall in love with yourself and with *your* talent. Find a way to score well with *your* stuff. A lot of gifted people don't do that. For many players, it means they better get good at kissing their own butt once a round starts until it is finished. Golf itself will try to beat you up, so you better not be beating yourself up, too, or it will kill your game.

It's like the story that Steph Curry told to *ESPN The Magazine* about his college coach, Bob McKillop. "He gave me all the confidence in the world in terms of what I could be, in terms of being a man," Curry said. "He told me when I was a freshman that I had license to shoot any shot I wanted, but I'd have to work for it. Even when I failed early in my freshman year, he stayed in my ear because he saw my potential before I did." This is so true of golfers. If you don't have a coach telling you how good you will be, you have to tell it to yourself. Part of your job is to get a coach who believes in you, and if you can have a team of people, another part of your job is to get the whole team to share in your vision. You might have a fitness trainer, a nutritionist, a sport psychologist, and you've got to get them all to see what *you're* seeing. Don't wait for them all to see it. Build a culture around you and get everyone to embrace that culture. It takes some time to do that. I think of the great

Billie Holiday song lyric "Mama may have, Papa may have / But God bless the child that's got his own."

Your thinking about yourself has to be consistent with what you want and where you want to go, not where you've been. It's okay for you and your teacher to sit down and analyze what went wrong, but then you need to go to work to improve on it. Don't let it become your image of yourself. Your thinking has to be based on where you want to go and what you want to do the next time.

Call it positive thinking. Call it faith. Call it belief. Call it feeling destined. Call it optimism. Those are things you can—and should—create about yourself. But I promise you, I've seen a lot of people in my lifetime who are absolutely convinced that they're going to get screwed in life, no matter what they do. No matter how much they practice, no matter how hard they try, they don't believe in their ability and think it's just not going to happen for them, and it becomes a self-fulfilling prophecy. They end up giving up on themselves. They never get to find out if they were destined for greatness; they never gave it a chance to happen. Do not let that happen to you. Your self-fulfilling prophecy should be something positive and based on what you want.

Coaches in other sports are always planting seeds in their players' heads to set up a self-fulfilling prophecy. In basketball, if a player is short, we tell them you've got a big heart. You might very well have to do that for yourself, plant a seed in your own head. Brooks Koepka says that during the week of a major, while he's lost in his own bubble, he reminds himself, "I want to make my mark in history. I've got it in my mind that I'm great at golf, and I've put the most time and energy into it, and I'm certainly going to believe in myself."

It's okay to acknowledge that recently your game is lousy, but you can't allow yourself to think that it means *you* are lousy and you are never going to be any good. Your attitude has to be "When I put it all together, I will play great golf." You have to feel entitled, you need to feel deserving. It's like the statement the tour player Max Homa told *Golf Digest* after he won a tournament at the end of a season: "My caddie, Joe Greiner,

How Jordan Spieth Raised His Game

After his 2017 victory in the British Open, Jordan Spieth said that he had been struggling with his swing. His caddie, Michael Greller, reminded him of something important. "I had just spent a day with Michael Phelps and Michael Jordan, who are the greatest ever in their sports, which I am not," Spieth said. "But my caddie told me I am just like them, which I am not because I am not the best ever, but it got me to believe in myself, and when you believe that you are the best, it's almost as impactful as if you are, so it helped me a lot."

recently told me I had to stop saying, 'I suck.' All golfers say it: 'That sucks, this sucks, you suck.' But I decided to not do it anymore. If you tell yourself you suck all the time, eventually you're going to think you really do suck."

Some teachers can be detrimental to your self-belief. You need to stay away from those. Some teachers at the beginning of the first lesson want to put you on video, then they show you all the things they think are wrong with your swing. If you are too good a student and totally buy in to everything your teacher is telling you, you'll probably start filling your head with doubt and fear. You might need a little of that, but some of the best teachers don't want their pupils to look at their swings on video. I've had players who've been on tour for ten years come to me and say they went to a lesson with so-and-so, and the teacher told them there is no way you can play on tour with that swing. And the players said they never went back for another lesson with that teacher because they had played on tour for ten years *with that swing*. So don't let anybody tell you something that will destroy your self-belief. In an ideal situation, your teacher will tell you what you need to do to improve your swing and never mention what is wrong.

Golf is a participant sport. It is one of the only sports that the average person watches on TV and also plays. It's not true of football, baseball, basketball, NASCAR, and most other spectator sports. One way to create your own self-fulfilling prophecy about your golf game is by watching golf on TV *as a player*, not as a fan. So much of the televised golf commentary is designed to create excitement and drama. The TV producers and commentators are trying to create anxiety. Commentators bring up all sorts of things that tour players are not thinking about. The commentators tell you about how to mess up a shot, or what a good or bad decision is, or where you can't miss. That is *not* what the player is usually thinking. I recommend you watch with the sound turned off and pretend you are one of the players in one of the final groups, so you are mentally engaged. Tell yourself, *Okay, I'm one back with two holes to play. What is my game plan? What if I start one back and after five holes I'm two behind? Am I going to remain cool and calm? Am I going to keep in the present tense, stay with my game plan, play one shot at a time, and stick to my routine? What if I started one ahead and now I'm four ahead after six holes? What am I going to be doing coming down the stretch? Am I going to look at leaderboards, or am I going to stay in the moment? When am I likely going to start thinking ahead and get ahead of myself?* You can learn a lot of good things if you are actively engaged as a player. But if you are just watching as a fan, you might learn a lot of bad habits and bad thinking processes.

Also, you wouldn't like it if someone picked on you all the time, so why would you constantly pick on yourself and pick apart your own game? You need to believe in yourself as if you were your own best friend. Don't lose the tournament or match before it starts just because you don't believe in yourself. Don't lose to the name of the tournament, or to the names of the people you are paired with, or to the names of the people who are in the field. I tell a lot of the younger people I work with to stop going on their computer to see who is in the field of a tournament they are about to play in. Make the other players irrelevant to you. Make them invisible and immaterial to you. They have nothing to do with you. You need to learn to play against yourself and the course. It is one of the beauties of the game of golf. Remember, you are going out there to shoot the best score you can shoot. You have a much better chance of doing that if you make sure you believe in yourself and your abilities and play your game. That's how you create your own self-fulfilling prophecy.

CHAPTER 3

Harnessing the Power of Persistence

A few times in my life I laid off two to three days. It seemed like it took me a month to three months to get back those three days when I took a rest. It's a tough situation. I had to practice all the time.

—Ben Hogan

Hogan is considered perhaps the best ball-striker of all time and won nine major championships, including the Masters, US Open, and British Open in 1953. After turning professional, he spent nine lean years, going broke twice, before he won his first tournament.

First of all, as I've stated elsewhere in this book and many times to the players I work with, to achieve everything you want in the game, you have to decide that you *will* outwork everyone else. There is no specific answer as to how hard you must work at your game or how many hours a day you must commit to practicing, but you must be willing to do whatever it takes to get as good as you dream of getting. It is different for everyone. You can call it patience, dogged determination, perseverance, or simply old-fashioned persistence. Whatever it is, to make your next shot your best shot every time, to achieve your wildest dreams and become the best golfer you can possibly be, you need to totally love what you are doing, stick with it through thick and thin, and be committed no matter what obstacles are thrown at you. It's like the Mars rover that took years to conceive and design, overcame various logistical setbacks, and then required seven months to travel from earth to its destination. Appropriately, it is named *Perseverance*. Likewise, staying the course is easier when things are going your way and coaches and others around you are constantly giving you praise and encouragement, especially if you are seeing promising results. But what if you're not? What if no matter how hard you're practicing your full swing, how many hours you're working on your short game, and how many days you've devoted to improving your skills, your scores still don't reflect your work ethic, and you are not improving? What if, over and over, your next shot is not even close to being your best shot?

This is when you have to decide how badly you want to chase your dream. This is when you have to tell yourself that you knew the challenge was going to be difficult, and that was a big part of the appeal. This is the time to suck it up and renew or double your commitment level. This is when the challenge must excite you even more and light a fire inside you. You

My dad always told me that if you want to be a champion, you have to be willing to do things other people are not willing to do.

—Johnny Miller

either talk yourself into going forward or talk yourself into retreating and giving up. You must win this battle. But when there is no progress, you cannot allow yourself to start feeling sorry for yourself or start second-guessing your commitment. This is not the time to begin questioning whether your efforts will ever pay off, or questioning your ability to ever get better. Continuing during difficult moments is the essence of persistence.

But to continue, you better know what your priorities are, what's important to you, and what kind of commitment you need to make and be willing to work for. In golf, numerous players toiled for years in obscurity before finally breaking through. Padraig Harrington was unheralded as a junior golfer in Ireland. He certainly wasn't a child prodigy. He wasn't recruited to an American college on a golf scholarship, as are so many talented European players today. Yet through persistence and dedication over many years, he became one of the most successful international players of his time, winning three major championships over a thirteen-month period, thirty-one professional titles so far, and becoming the 2021 European Ryder Cup captain.

Pat Bradley also was not a standout junior player in her native Massachusetts, and she only met with sporadic success as an amateur and in college at Florida International University.

The Real Heroics Take Place When No One Is Watching

You might know that Bill Russell, the legendary basketball star, won two NCAA championships and eleven NBA championships, the all-time record. But did you know he was cut from his junior high school basketball team and almost cut from his high school team? Fortunately, a coach saw promise and told him to work hard on his fundamentals. So he spent countless hours working on the basics. His footwork, his balance, his ballhandling, his defensive skills. All top golfers on tour do the same thing, spending lonely hours every day—day after day—honing their fundamentals so they are automatic in competition, but average fans don't see all the work they do. "I came against long odds from the ghetto to the very top of my profession," Russell says today. "I was not immediately good at basketball. It did not come easy. It came as a result of a lot of hard work and self-sacrifice."

When she first joined the tour in 1974, her victories were far and few between. She finished second six times in 1976, the year she finally won a tour event, the Girl Talk Classic. She started working with me about that time, and I soon learned that she was the epitome of perseverance and setting high expectations. She was extremely demanding of herself, always striving for something greater. Nothing would stop her from working on her game. She did it every day with the utmost commitment and dedication to improvement. She finally met with major success at the 1981 US Women's Open. But her breakout year was 1986, when she won three majors and came close in the fourth, finishing tied for fifth at the US Women's Open. She also won the money title that year, and as we continued to work together, she became the first LPGA player to cross the $2 million, $3 million, and $4 million milestones in career earnings. She went on to win thirty-one times on the LPGA Tour, which qualified her for the LPGA Hall of Fame, an amazing achievement, and was the 2000 Solheim Cup captain. "Commitment was the key," she once said. "You can have success, failure, setback, and defeat and rise above it."

Justin Rose is regarded as one of the greatest players of the current generation, having won the 2013 US Open at Merion, finished second in three other majors, won twenty-four professional events, and won a gold medal at the 2016 Olympics in Rio de Janeiro. Yet, during his first year on tour after turning professional, he missed the cut in his first twenty-one tournaments! Through sheer hard work and determination, he became one of the best golfers on the planet and even achieved the No. 1 ranking in 2018.

Golf is not always a fair game. It can be grueling, it can be cruel, and it can be tough. However, golf's unfairness is one of the reasons it is so alluring. To become as good as you can be at golf will take an unbelievable amount of perseverance. You will ask yourself, "Is it worth it? Is it ever going to pay off? Is my game ever going to fall into place?" You will struggle at times, you will work hard and might go backward, eventually followed by a jump forward. The game requires a lot of hanging in there and stick-to-itiveness. It's not usually a smooth ride. You can plan on getting beaten up a lot. Dream big, but realize that the road will be filled with bumps. The game will try to beat you up. It will try to convince you that you don't have what it takes. It will try to make you question yourself and your future. It will try to make you wonder, *Is it meant to be or is it all for naught?*

You must remember that when you are chasing a dream and going for greatness, it's all about possibilities, not about probabilities. You are taking a chance. You are committing to going for it. You are pursuing something special, something challenging. Most people cannot handle the difficulty, the setbacks, the alone moments lost in their own thoughts, wondering if the effort is worth it. You must always be able to come back with a reason why it *is* worth it. This is why some people say there is not much difference between being totally committed and being addicted. At times, it will feel as if golf almost owns you.

Don't Ever Give Up

Stan Wawrinka, the second-best tennis player ever from Switzerland (after Roger Federer), has this verse from the poet Samuel Beckett tattooed on his left arm: "Ever tried. Ever failed. No matter. Try Again. Fail again. Fail better." Wawrinka has won three Grand Slam titles (the 2014 Australian Open, the 2015 French Open, and the 2016 US Open). In each final he defeated the current No. 1 player in the world. He has also amassed more than $34 million in prize money.

In your journey to the top, there will be days when you feel as if you have conquered the world, and there will be days of doubt and fighting through fear. You can always be in control of your thoughts and your emotions, but you cannot always control the times when your game doesn't fall into place. You just have to keep working *until* it falls into place. You must get through the days when you are hitting it great but your score doesn't reflect that. Or the days when your short game is great but the ball will not go where you are looking. So a lot of success depends on how good you get at handling your frustrations and the doubts in your mind, especially those planted there by so-called experts. Can you get through the emotions that go with the fear of failure, the tears, the feeling sorry for yourself, the sadness, the ridicule, the wondering if it is worth it?

If you want to be a great success story at whatever level you play, you're going to be putting your name, your image, and your reputation on the line every time you show up to compete. You have to be willing to post your score for others to scrutinize, judge, and evaluate. They might rip you apart. They might praise you. You must be able to take the bad with

Can You Be Well-to-Do and Still Be Hungry?

When I was a kid, we didn't have enough money to join a country club. It never crossed my mind that we should. It was fine with me. But I thought we were pretty tough guys because we were poor and hungry. The kids from my side of the tracks, man, that was our calling card. Playing football, we were going to beat the kids on the other side of town because we were poor and hungry. Fifty years later, I've come to realize that it's way more impressive to be well-to-do and hungry—and motivated. It's easier to be poor and hungry. The question is, can you be brought up with most everything handed to you on a silver platter and be hungry and disciplined?

the good. Most athletes eventually learn that as long as they are "talking about *me*, I must be doing something right and I am on my way to the top." But getting to this point does not always come easily.

You will have to have your ego under control. You will have to know who you are, what you're all about, and where you are going. I've never met an athlete who didn't have some insecurities, but you have to constantly work on not being overly sensitive and learning how to be secure with yourself. You will need thick skin and hardened emotions. Your opinion of yourself must mean more to you than the opinions of others.

The road to the top will at times require blind faith. If you are not willing to take the risk of ridicule, then you will not get to the other side, where you are praised as a champion. You need to understand that this is what it's all about. It is not always wine and roses. It is not only accepting this reality, it is about embracing this aspect of your journey. At some point in your development, you will advance to where the competition is really good. Where no one stinks. You look around and see that everyone can play. You will play great, but then someone will do even better. That is when the mental and emotional challenge becomes a huge deciding factor in your career development. If you are a late bloomer, the challenge might be even greater, but no matter how great the challenge, you must be able to sustain your daily work ethic and hold on to your hopes and dreams. This is so much of what being persistent and stubborn with your commitment is all about.

Some people perceive stubbornness as something negative. But when it comes to commitment and sticking with your teacher and being dedicated to what you are working on, being stubborn is a good thing.

You have to keep practicing diligently, even when your game is a struggle. You have to be able to persevere and know that you just haven't put the pieces of the puzzle together yet, and know that when you do, you will have a blast showing off your game. You must have faith that your day will come. This is what great success stories are all about. Unless you are that can't-miss kid who has won everything he has played in since he was six years old, this is what your story is going to be like. You must be prepared for it. You must welcome it and embrace the challenge.

Love the difficulty. Take pride in being tougher and more resilient than others. This will make your story a great one that will inspire others like you in the future. You must welcome going through the fire that burns away the impurities and makes you into something special. If you let the setbacks hurt you, it *can* destroy you if you let it. It can keep you from your destiny. It can cause you to convince yourself that you don't have it, and it was not meant to be.

You *have* to be able to fight through it. You must persevere and patiently and diligently hold on to your dreams, even when so many others ask you why you put so much into your game. When they ask you if it is worth the time and energy you are devoting to this game, you must battle through.

Getting Started in Golf

At least for the first seven to ten years, you better have the mentality that you are going to outwork everybody else who plays your sport, and that certainly applies to young golfers who want to be great. Because I think it takes that long for most people to develop skill in all parts of this game. Then after seven to ten years, you can start working smarter and better and be more efficient with your practice. But for the first seven to ten years, if everyone else is outworking you, then you're going to be in trouble long-term. In golf, everything is earned, and nothing is given. As Tom Kite once told me, in pro golf your career starts all over every day.

Disappointments are just a part of your quest. You must be able to keep your progress in perspective. You are on a mission to see how good you can get at this game that you say you love. And you're going to get up every day filled with passion because this is what you love doing. No other reason is needed.

You do not waste your time worrying about where your game is going, or when it is going to fall into place, or wondering why you are not shooting great scores now, given how hard you have been working. You have to just get up every day doing the thing you love doing, going back to the practice tee, going back to the short-game area, working on your mind, working on your emotions, developing yourself and your game.

You're not going to let even regular setbacks stand in your way. Nothing will stop you or hold you back. You are determined and committed. You have a plan and you will honor your plan and commitment until your game falls into place. You understand that not only is failure not bad, it is the stuff that

How Mike Weir Never Gave Up

Mike Weir, whom I worked with a lot, is a great example of perseverance. He missed the PGA Tour School five times. "I can remember many times that I was missing cut after cut on the Australian Tour, and I was by myself and didn't have any money," he once said. "You're out on the range by yourself practicing until you can't see a shot five feet in front of you." Mike finally got on tour, but lost his card in his first year. Then he went back to the Tour School and won it. He went on to win eight PGA Tour events, played in six World Cups, five Presidents Cups, and won the 2003 Masters (the only Canadian man to ever win a major) and the Tour Championship. After that, he struggled again with his game, but now is enjoying life on the Champions Tour.

greatness is made of. This might not make a great story, but it is the truth about greatness. It is crucial that you understand this as you go on your journey of discovering your potential. You cannot care if it comes hard for you. You cannot care if your progress is slow. You cannot care if you feel as if you're working harder than others who are at the moment playing better than you. It is not about how big you are. It is not about how long you hit it. It is not about whether you won everything as a kid. It is about how badly you want to be great. It is about refusing to give up on your dreams. It is about never quitting. It is about chasing your dreams, having a ball while on the journey, and being proud that you are willing to go for it.

You persevere because you know that this is your destiny. This is what you were born to do. There will be heartbreaking moments, but you realize they are just the flip side of great moments in your life. And the hurt makes the best moments all the better. So you must keep moving forward. You just keep taking it one step at a time, one day at a time. Some days you do it for pure joy. Some days you do it with a chip on your shoulder to prove all the doubters wrong. Some days you simply enjoy the loneliness of grinding it out in the practice area. However you do it, you find a way, every day, to bring the energy and the passion to practice. It has always been this way. It will always be this way for most people. There is no shortcut.

Can you persist day after day? Can you keep the passion? It is your choice to make every day. You must fight for your ideas and your dreams. You must keep chasing your destiny if you truly want to discover what is possible. It is *your* life. It is *your* career. It is *your* game. And it is up to *you* to find a way. *Your* way. *Your* story. This is what learning how to win and being great is all about. It is about winning the battle with yourself every day, but especially during the tough times. As you will find out in the coming chapters, persistence is a crucial piece of the puzzle of putting your golf game together. It is a key part of the story, but it is most certainly not the whole story.

CHAPTER 4

How Tom Kite Got the Passion—and Keeps It

I wouldn't let Tommy [Kite] watch Ben [Crenshaw] take a lesson or Ben watch Tommy.

—Harvey Penick

Dr. Bob Rotella: Since the early 1970s, it's fair to say that World Golf Hall of Famer Tom Kite has had a reputation of being one of the most dedicated and hardworking players at any level of the game. I've been advising Tom for almost forty years, starting in the early 1980s, and he's certainly one of the players I admire most. That's why for this chapter I asked Tom to give his thoughts on what he had to do to achieve his greatest successes in the game. Growing up, Tom often played in the shadow of a player who was two years younger but physically more mature, Ben Crenshaw. Which is a meaningful story for kids today: just because someone is bigger and more successful than you right now does not mean it will always be that way, especially if you work hard and dream big. After he tied for the NCAA individual championship with Crenshaw in 1972, and then was the PGA Tour Rookie of the Year, Tom still had some lean years before he met with his noteworthy accomplishments. He persevered, and eventually he amassed an amazing record: he became the PGA Tour's Player of the Year in 1989, was the year's leading money winner twice, was the all-time leading money winner for nine straight years, won the Vardon Trophy twice, played on seven Ryder Cup teams (accumulating an incredible 15-9-4 record), was the Ryder Cup captain in 1997, won the 1992 US Open at Pebble Beach, and won nineteen times on the PGA Tour and ten times on the PGA Champions Tour. Regarding the longevity of his career, he is the only player to have made the cut in the first four US Opens played at Pebble Beach—in 1972, 1982, 1992, and 2000. So what does that tell you? Somehow, Tom has been able to keep his passion for golf alive and well over the years. He has reached for incredibly high dreams, and he has been able to achieve them. Here's what he told me recently when I asked him to talk about his work ethic, his passion for the game, and his ultimate success.

Tom Kite: "Well, in my case it started out by having good parents! They gave me an opportunity to do what I wanted to do, and certainly Mom and Dad were awesome. My dad coming out of the Great Depression and knowing how difficult everything was then, he had the mindset that if you're going to ever achieve anything, you'll have to outwork everybody. I think that was the lesson I learned from him. Whether you're an immigrant

HOW TOM KITE GOT THE PASSION—AND KEEPS IT   53

coming into this country looking for opportunity, or you have a less than ideal family life or are in an economic situation that puts you behind the eight ball, those are the people who tend to achieve great success by outworking everybody else. When I started to play golf as a kid and showed that I wanted to pursue that, Dad taught me that if you're going to be good at something where very, very few achieve great success at a high level, you're going to have to outwork a bunch of people. He instilled that in me early on.

How Tom Kite Helped Other Players—and Himself

When I first started working with Tom Kite, he started winning. A couple of years go by and he suggested that we get two or three young tour players to come to Florida, and we could spend two or three days talking about attitude, and how to be really successful on tour. So I got Davis Love III, Brad Faxon, and David Frost to get together with Tom and me. We're not in the first meeting for one minute and Davis says to Tom, "Okay, so you start working with Doc and he starts helping you win. Why would you invite us down here to share everything you're learning that's helping *you* play better?" Tom looked at Davis and said, "Well, that's pretty simple. It really helped me to have Ben Crenshaw beating my brains out as a kid. I don't know if I'd be as good a player as I became if I didn't have Crenshaw pushing me and beating me." And Tom said, "The better you guys play, it's going to force me to play better, and the better I play, it's going to force you guys to play better. That's what competition is all about. And we're going to just all help each other and see how good we can get. And when we're on the road and Doc's not with us, we can sit down and talk together about it."

I thought Tom's response was brilliant, and it showed a healthy confidence in himself. He wanted to see how good he could get. It's like Gary Player's line "I want to beat people when they're playing well, not when they're playing poorly."

"However, it wasn't a tough push for me because I was doing something that I really enjoyed. I was lucky in that I had found something I loved to do. I loved playing golf, and I loved playing golf well, and I loved competing. Dad kept stressing that if I were to excel and improve at my craft, it would need to become part of my MO. You see, I also loved to practice. I was quoted in *Golf Digest*'s fiftieth anniversary book [published in 2000] as saying, 'When I was eleven years old or thirteen years old, I did the same thing that I do now. Hit balls from morning till night.' It's safe to say that's been true my entire career! Even today at seventy years of age, I like hitting golf balls. That's just something I like to do. The term *work* has a negative connotation, but I never considered practicing golf as work. It's not drudgery. But in terms of time, I would say probably nobody's hit more golf balls than I have. I know that Ben Hogan was the very first really big practicer, but he had to wait while his caddie who was shagging for him brought the balls back. We have all our golf balls just given to us on the range. If for no other reason than *that*, I know I've hit more golf balls than Mr. Hogan. Gary Player was the other really prolific practicer. If I'm not the one who's hit the most golf balls, I'd say Gary is. Fortunately, my body has held up pretty well. I had one little session with a bulging disk in the early nineties, and a couple of operations on my shoulder and knee in my sixties, but otherwise I've been injury-free."

Dr. Bob Rotella: I asked Tom how he first got to know the legendary Harvey Penick, who was such a fortuitous influence on his life and his golf.

Tom Kite: "Fortunately, when I was twelve years old, my dad was transferred from Dallas down to Austin, and there was a great teacher there—Mr. Penick—who was teaching a lot of really good players in the central-Texas area. There were so many single-digit handicap players around that, even though I thought I was pretty good, I found out I wasn't very good yet. If I were going to try to compete with those guys, I had to really work hard. I guarantee you there were more single-digit handicaps in Austin—men and women—than probably in any city in America, even those ten times as big as Austin. It was a great community to learn how to play golf. And everybody in Austin took lessons from Harvey, including a lot of the other professionals around. His values and his skill in teaching transferred down.

"You combine some great instruction with great competition and a desire to be able to compete at that level, it encourages you to continue to work harder, and I jumped on that. For some reason, I liked to win. For me, that was the fun part of it and kept me motivated. I relished getting the trophies, and getting the accolades, and having people tell me that I had done good things.

"Harvey taught everybody differently. He didn't have a method. It wasn't cookie-cutter for him. He had some simple fundamentals that he stuck with. Like, 'If you don't have a good grip, you don't want a good swing.' In other words, if you have a bad grip, then you need a swing that compensates for it. He gave his students what they needed, and consequently, all his students got better.

"To this day, I remember my first lesson from Harvey. We had just moved down to Austin and I was twelve years old and feeling pretty good about my future. We were in a cart driving up the hill from the pro shop to the practice tee at the Austin Country Club, and he said, 'I'm looking forward to working with you, Tommy, and with some practice and hard work you should be able to make the junior high golf team.' Of course, I had already decided that I was going on the PGA Tour. I said, 'Mr. Penick, I'd like to go on tour one of these days.' He said, 'I understand that, Tommy, but first we've got to make the junior high golf team. And then we've got to make the high school golf team. Then we've got to make the university golf team. Eventually we'll get there, but we've got to do this step by step by step.' So that was a really good first lesson. Harvey was making the point that it's great to have those high aspirations—Doc calls them dreams—but I shouldn't get ahead of myself. And to reach my goals, I would have to work really hard. Harvey always loved seeing people excel, but he knew to be great required a lot of dedication."

Dr. Bob Rotella: I wanted to make a point about Tom Kite's work ethic. If you go to many of today's country clubs, a lot of young kids think they're working hard on their games. In fact, some lazy people think they're really working. So I asked Tom to talk us through what a typical day was like for him growing up.

Tom Kite: "In the summer, I would get up early, my dad would drop me off at seven forty-five on his way to work [for the IRS]. It would be just me and the guys mowing the greens on the golf course. Harvey would be there. I had the whole driving range to myself for an hour or so. About nine o'clock my buddies would show up. They'd warm up for a few minutes and we'd go play. After eighteen holes, we'd have lunch, they'd jump in the pool, and then we'd play more. Usually I'd practice instead of being in the pool. Then Dad would show up after work and we'd play nine more holes. A lot of days I'd play forty-five holes, always walking, carrying my bag. If you read Harvey's books, you know how he felt about carts. We never rode on the course. I don't even ride in a cart today. Dad and I would come home

Tom Kite's Secret to Success on Tour

Years ago, I'm at the Byron Nelson Championship with Tom Kite. On Tuesday of the tournament week, we had lunch with the club's teaching pro, who ran their junior program and wanted to ask Tom some questions. The pro, who was very direct, said to Tom, "I know you struggled some your rookie year on tour [Kite missed the cut in about half the tournaments he entered but was still named Rookie of the Year]. What did you do that year when you missed the cut in a tournament?"

Tom didn't take offense. He looked at the pro and said, "Well, I decided that the best practice facilities I could find were right there at the tour site. So I got up really early on

Saturday and Sunday, and I was on the range by six-thirty or seven in the morning. I'd stay there till twelve-thirty or one o'clock and get a great practice session in. I would get a quick sandwich, shower, and then I would follow the last group on Saturday and Sunday because I wanted to see what they were doing that I wasn't doing on a course I had just played. I wanted to observe their strategy. I wanted to see what they were hitting off the tees. I wanted to see how they played the par 5s. I learned a lot."

The pro looked at Tom. "Who told you to do that?"

Tom said nobody, it just made good sense to him. I thought that was brilliant, and it was probably one reason Tom was the tour's leading money winner twice and was the first $6 million man in career prize money (he also was the first to reach $7 million, $8 million, and $9 million in career earnings).

and have dinner. We built a putting green in the backyard with some portable lights. It wasn't a great green, but it was okay, and I would putt after dinner. So it was pretty much golf for me, sunup to sundown. During the school year, as soon as I got out of class, I'd foot it to the golf course as quick as I could, and I'd play or practice until dark, again always walking.

"I've always contended that to play the PGA Tour you have to be a great walker. You're walking six or seven miles, day after day, at a relatively brisk pace. The marshals and standard-bearers are always surprised how quickly we walk from shot to shot. I believe walking, rather than riding, especially on the senior tour, has contributed to my longevity in my career. I never have liked riding in a cart. Even today when I play with my buddies, some of whom I played junior high golf with, we still walk all the time. I think that's a great lesson for juniors. Don't get in the habit of riding in a cart. Your golf will suffer for it."

Dr. Bob Rotella: I asked Tom to describe in more detail his practice sessions when he was growing up.

Tom Kite: "Harvey was huge on the short game. He stressed that a lot. The chipping green, the practice bunker, and the putting green were pretty accessible for that day. Because of Harvey and his teaching, the membership made sure there was a great short-game area. The putting green was large and in great shape. It was tilted a bit, like an old-style green, back to front. So I got to practice uphill, downhill, left-breakers, right-breakers. There were a few little mounds, but not much. It was great for perfecting those touch shots and your imagination, with a lot of areas to hit chip shots.

"Even when I got on tour, my practice sessions were designed for whatever my game needed at the time. I never counted golf balls or thought of percentages of time, but it was probably close to fifty-fifty full swing versus short game. As a kid, my practice was always dominated by games. Harvey always wanted us to play competitions. Chipping competitions, putting competitions, bunker competitions. If there wasn't anybody around to compete against, then you competed against yourself. You put yourself under pressure to beat the other guy, even for a dime. I was always trying to do different things around the practice green, hitting different pitch shots, unusual chip shots, experimenting with difficult and easy lies. Anything to make it interesting. I hit a lot of shots on the range, but seldom did I hit the same shot two or three times in a row. I was always trying to do something different and replicate playing situations.

"Golf is a complicated game, and it's hard to learn, and there is a lot to know. To be a really good player, you need to understand different grasses, different types of sand, different kinds of equipment. All good players have an understanding of those things. They might not understand the teaching of the golf swing, but they understand *their* swing. I wanted to understand everything there was about the game. I just loved learning about it. Hence, I sought out information and instruction from various teachers and sources. Then I decided what was good for me and what I needed to use to always get better. Over time, I found out that some of the stuff I learned was applicable to my game and some wasn't. Some ideas just didn't work and didn't fit. Usually with the consultation of Harvey, I was able to figure out what was best for my game—what stuff I should spend my time on and what would only waste my time."

Dr. Bob Rotella: Clearly, Tom has met with some amazing successes throughout his career, namely winning the Vardon Trophy two years in a row (1981 and '82), winning Player of the Year (1989), and winning the 1992 US Open. I asked him how he stayed motivated and how he was able to keep driving himself after those accomplishments.

Tom Kite: "Well, I just liked to play well. It's not any more complicated than that. Winning was my big motivator. I'm not a real goal-setter, in terms of short-term goals and long-term goals. But every day when I get up, I want to improve my golf game. Always have. I could say the obvious things that motivated me: making Ryder Cup teams, winning tournaments, winning majors. But you can't always control winning. You can control playing as well as you can. So every day I would just do what I thought would help me become a better player, be it working out, watching my diet, or getting enough rest—something Doc really helped me understand the importance of, and something I did *not* get from my father, who did not have an appreciation for taking time off and seeing the benefit of that. Everything I did was with the idea of being a better golfer."

Dr. Bob Rotella: Tom played in twenty-two US Opens until he finally won one. Before he won, I wondered how he kept believing in himself and getting excited going to each US Open and thinking he would win.

Tom Kite: "Every tournament I went into, the goal was to win. That was the expectation, whether it be the Fourth of July tournament when I was an amateur here in Austin or the US Open or the Masters. The ultimate goal was to really play well and have a chance to win the golf tournament. Obviously, some tournaments are more important than others, but in terms of the way I prepared, I tried to do very little differently."

Dr. Bob Rotella: What has always impressed me about Tom is that when he won a tournament, he got up the next day and went back to work, and when he didn't win a tournament, he did the same thing. No difference.

Tom Kite: "Yes, that's pretty much true. Okay, I won the tournament yesterday, but what can I do to get better *today*, because that was yesterday? That's past tense. I always viewed it that way. When I won the US Open at Pebble in '92, the very next tournament was at Westchester, on the other side of the country. I wanted to win Westchester. I really, really wanted to win that week just to kind of back it up. I didn't win, but I finished fourth. I guess it's because I'm passionate about what I do. I love seeing passion that way in other players. I enjoy the passion. For example, after everything I've read and learned about Bryson DeChambeau [2020 US Open champion], I love this kid. I love his passion for the game and for getting as good as he can get. Here's a kid who's doing everything he can to get better, including experimenting with a forty-eight-inch driver. His passion is admirable."

Dr. Bob Rotella: When we talk about passion, a lot of people think about being single-minded, and a lot of kids feel they have to sacrifice and give up things.

Tom Kite: "Well, the line 'You can have it all' is impossible. Nobody can do it all. But the trick is to find out what you want to do and what's important to you. In my case, the important thing for me was how was I going to become a better golfer. When my buddies were spending two hours in the pool, that was time I could be hitting golf balls. I was practicing my chipping or my putting or my wedge game or my bunker shots. That's all I cared about. The pool was not high on my priority list."

Dr. Bob Rotella: Tom has had his share of ups and downs, and even heartbreak, in competition. For example, he lost the 1990 US Open at Oak Hill after leading going into the final round. How did he come back from that adversity, keep a positive attitude, and two years later win the US Open?

Tom Kite: "I didn't perform as well as I felt like I should have under those circumstances, and so, not wanting to do that again, I started trying to figure out what I needed to do. I was so good mentally that week at Oak Hill and got myself in position to win early in the fourth round. And then I hit a bad shot on number 5, and it cost me the tournament, and I wasn't able to recover. That was a swing breakdown. Shortly after that tournament, I started making some swing changes so that wouldn't happen again. Always before, I could say, 'You know, I lost my concentration' or 'I wasn't tough enough mentally.' But that Open at Oak Hill, that was like a two-by-four across the side of the head. Because I was so good mentally that week and so good emotionally, and I was pretty good physically, but I could absolutely say my swing broke down, and it broke down at the worst time. I had gotten myself in position to win the tournament and hit one bad shot.

You Must Adapt to Changes in the Game

Adapting to changing conditions and the way playing golf has evolved can be difficult for many players, especially those who are older and have had success doing it their way. I've seen some players question why certain rules have been changed. They get hung up on it, to the detriment of their own games. Changes include course setups to make it easier to bomb the ball off the tee or tighter lies around the greens, or US Open–type rough around the greens that eliminates chipping. Allowing the armlock putting technique while disallowing anchoring the putter into your chest is another example that might seem unfair. Or thinner faces on fairway woods that allow players with faster swing speeds to hit those clubs appreciably farther without losing accuracy.

I tell the players I work with that they don't make the rules, but they have to play by them. Rather than complaining about what might seem like a hindrance to your specific strengths, you must adapt and find the positives and get on with your game. It's like when I played lacrosse in high school and college, they came out with the plastic stick. I resisted changing for months, which was holding me back. Finally, I went to the plastic stick and couldn't believe how great it was. You might be hesitant to put a couple more hybrids in your bag, or to go to a third wedge, as Tom Kite did years ago. But if you don't embrace the changes of the modern game, you'll get left behind.

"I got some swing advice from John Rhodes and Jimmy McLean and took that back to Chuck Cook, whom I had been working with. I pulled these thoughts together and also went over it with Harvey. We tightened up my swing a lot and got out of that big reverse-C finish. I became much more consistent—and confident—under pressure. Keeping my left heel down and keeping my lower body more stable on the backswing, not only was I more consistent, my clubhead speed was faster. I picked up speed, I picked up distance, I controlled the ball better, I flighted it better, especially with my long irons and fairway woods."

Dr. Bob Rotella: I wondered if Tom had any further advice he would offer to younger golfers.

Tom Kite: "If I were giving advice to young kids who were just starting out and wanted to fulfill their dreams, I would tell them to always surround yourself—and hang out with—good people, and those who want to be really good players. Play with golfers who are a little better than you. That will encourage you to get even better. Learn everything you can about your craft. And that's not just swinging a golf club and your ability to score. You need to learn something about agronomy. Something about equipment. Fitness. Nutrition. The mental side. The emotional side. You need to understand what your body can handle. You need to study golf-course architecture. Different golf-course grasses and different types of sand. A solid understanding of these things will make your life so much easier. If you have a chance to talk with somebody who has gone through it—perhaps a tour player or a club professional—remember, there are no dumb questions. Golf is unique in that regard—most people are willing to share what they know and describe their experiences.

"Make sure you take care of your body. When I went on tour, I weighed a little over 170 pounds. But at the end of my first year, I weighed about 155. Being on the golf course all day long, as opposed to being in the classroom, I started burning a lot more calories. In the late seventies, after I'd been on tour four or five years, I began working out. I started trying to gain some distance and speed because I could see that was going to be very beneficial. And then the fitness van came out on tour. I became addicted to working out. With a trainer who understands how the body functions, I put on about fourteen pounds of muscle over the next few years. Now, I go in five days a week, for an hour and fifteen minutes. The workouts are a little different from fifteen years ago, but there is still an emphasis on flexibility, stability, and speed, and some strength to go with that. It's all functional training. No isolation training. We do lunges and squats till the cows come home.

"Vice versa, if you are older and want to stay competitive in the game, act like a kid. Adopt the attitude that the game is fun and not that important. You will enjoy yourself more and will be more successful. If you're even older, like me, you can look forward to starting to shoot your age, like Bob Toski and Gary Player, who shoot their age every time they play."

Dr. Bob Rotella: Tom has always been known as not only inquisitive, but also innovative. He pioneered the idea of adding a third wedge to his set on tour, so he could make fuller swings with the shots under one hundred yards and reduce or eliminate the hated half wedge. This is how that concept came about:

Tom Kite: "Dave Pelz [the noted short-game guru] gave me that idea. He's been a good friend and still lives in Austin. In the 1970s, he wanted to quantify as much as he could in golf and turn it into more science than art. Me being analytical, I liked a lot of that stuff. In 1979, Dave came up to me at tournament and said, 'Tom, you've got a good short game, but it needs to be a lot better. When you get inside one hundred yards, you're good, but you're not as good as you should be.' He said I should put a third, more-lofted wedge in my bag. I wasn't sure about the stats he was showing me. So the first five months of 1980, I charted every shot that I hit on a graph. Long, short, left, and right. I found that what Dave was saying was accurate: when I had a full shot, my pattern was left and right, not short and long. The misses on the graph were elliptical and horizontal. But as I got to about one hundred to one hundred twenty yards from the green, that pattern of misses was pretty much a perfect circle. When I got inside one hundred yards, and especially around forty and fifty yards, my misses were long and short, not left and right. My pattern was on the vertical axis. So I built a wedge that I could only hit seventy yards with a full swing—with the old ball. My old sand wedge was like ninety-seven yards.

"The first tournament I put it in play was the Western Open in 1980. I was doing drills every day, doing distance wedges. I had my caddie, Mike Carrick, calling numbers to me, as I was hitting wedges thirty, thirty-five, forty, forty-five, fifty yards. I got really good at it. My stroke average the second half of the year went down almost a stroke and half over what it had been the first half of the year. I became the leading money winner in 1981, leading the tour in stroke average on par 5s. It was because of that wedge. I just out-wedged everybody. At home, Dad would be out there on the range, and we'd lay towels out. He would yell out, 'Hit it to fifty,' and then he would yell, 'Fifty-two.' Next, he would yell out, 'Hit it to thirty,' and he would yell out, 'Twenty-nine.' I could do that all day, and sometimes I would. That's the perfect game, just like playing golf. Today, the lofts on my wedges are forty-nine, fifty-six, and sixty-one degrees. But I'm old-school. Most other players' pitching wedges are like my 9-iron."

Dr. Bob Rotella: On tour, I would often challenge Tom to a contest, the winner buying dinner. There'd be a flag out on the range at seventy yards. I'd say, "You've got ten balls. If you hit the flag with one of those balls, I buy dinner. If you fail to hit it, you buy dinner.' I bought dinner like every time. It was ridiculous. That pretty well sums up Tom Kite's talent, his worth ethic, his perseverance, and his passion for the game.

CHAPTER 5

Bouncing Back: Dealing with Adversity and Heartbreak

I learned how to win by losing and not liking it.

—Tom Watson

Watson led the 1974 US Open going into the final round, shot 79 and tied for fifth. Subsequently, he won eight major championships.

Your dream is about winning and succeeding, yet a lot of success is about rebounding from mistakes, setbacks, and disappointments. It's about coming back after you didn't perform. Heartbreaking losses happen to all competitors because everyone is human. This is not usually what people who are chasing dreams of greatness think of first. So much of success, however, is about who is best at *responding* to setbacks.

Mistakes that happen in big moments, prolonged struggle, and being questioned by others are all part of the journey. If you cannot deal with tough times effectively, you will never reach your potential. You cannot become a comeback kid. You cannot become a great story. To get through these times, learn from them, put them behind you, and ultimately achieve your dreams, you must decide that you will be strong emotionally. Even if, for example, you don't have length off the tee, you don't have a super-athletic build, other people aren't telling you that you have unbelievable talent, and you're not sure you will ever recover from whatever adversity or heartbreak you are dealing with, you can always be mentally tougher and more resilient than everyone else. It's one of the keys to always making your next shot your best shot.

I have seen a number of golfers develop a shot they hate—say, a severe hook. That shot frightens them on a hole with trouble on that side of the fairway. Don't allow yourself to hate that shot—learn how to play for it under certain situations. Because sooner or later you will need to be able to play that shot. Also, remember that you can hit a great shot and still make a double bogey, and you can hit a poor shot and still make a birdie. That's just part of the game, so always keep pushing yourself, no matter what happens. It's all part of dealing with misfortune.

If you want to be the best you can be, you must get great at *thriving* when faced with adversity. You must be able to anticipate that you *will* struggle along the way. You must be willing to welcome it, you must control your perception of it, and you must dictate how you will respond to it. You must learn to be proud of how you deal with tough times, and to be proud of how you respond. It will require having resolve, having determination, and having a strong work ethic. At times it will take an undying belief—true grit.

Numerous successful people have overcome tremendous odds, have faced repeated failures, could have buckled under the duress but chose not to and rose up to fulfill their wildest dreams. One was Abraham Lincoln. Many people think of Lincoln as one of the most successful figures to have ever walked the earth, and he did have a few successes leading up to the presidency. But there was never an individual who met with more failure for most of his life. Yet, he endured with an incredible self-belief, and a persistent will to succeed, simply because he *chose* to. Lincoln could have quit many times, but he didn't, and because he didn't quit, he became arguably the greatest president in the history of our country. Lincoln once said, "A sense of obligation to continue is present in all of us. A duty described is the duty of all of us. I felt a call to that Duty."

Lincoln's Determination to Overcome Adversity

Following is the adversity that Abraham Lincoln had the resolve to overcome: In 1831 he failed in business. In 1832 he was defeated for the legislature. In 1833 he experienced a second failure in business. In 1835 his sweetheart, Ann

Rutledge, died. In 1836 he suffered a nervous breakdown. In 1838 he was defeated for speaker. In 1840 he was defeated for elector. In 1843 he was defeated for Congress. In 1848 he was once again defeated for Congress. In 1855 he was defeated for the Senate. In 1856 he was defeated for vice president. In 1858 he was again defeated for the Senate. Finally, in 1860, he was elected president. "The path was worn and slippery," Lincoln once said. "My foot slipped from under me, knocking the other out of the way. But I recovered and said to myself, 'It's a slip and not a fall.'" This philosophy served him well, and he achieved incredible greatness.

Rather than a physical challenge, setbacks are an inner challenge, both mentally and emotionally. The good news is, if you respond properly, these experiences will make you stronger and make you appreciate the good times all the more. Setbacks are simply opportunities to prove to yourself what you are all about, a chance to find out how tough you are on the inside. These moments keep you humble, but also test your belief in yourself. These are all-important lessons on your journey.

No matter how bad you hurt at times, no matter the heartbreak, you have to get through times that are challenging. Have you made a crucial mistake at the worst time? Everybody has done that. Can you forgive yourself after? It's how you handle it and react that matters. That's what mental toughness is all about. I often point to a great example of this in college basketball. In 1982, the legendary basketball coach at Georgetown, John Thompson, against North Carolina had a chance to win his first NCAA National Championship. Freddie Brown was a sophomore point guard for Georgetown. With twelve seconds left, Michael Jordan hit a jump shot to put Carolina ahead, 63–62. As Brown got to the top of the key with the ball, nobody was guarding him. That kind of freaked him out—along with the enormity of the situation. Carolina's James Worthy was standing to the side at half-court, strangely guarding nobody. Freddie turned and passed the ball backward to Worthy, who was shocked but dribbled down the court until he got fouled and the game was basically over. That was UNC coach Dean Smith's first National Championship. After the final buzzer, I noticed that Thompson went straight to Freddie Brown and gave him a bear hug and said something to him. So the next day I wanted to see if anybody would interview Brown and what Freddie might say. Sure enough, a television reporter caught up to him. Freddie said, "Coach Thompson told me that he loved me and there were many things in life way more important than winning or losing a basketball game. It really meant a lot to me and helped me deal with it, because it was the most heartbreaking thing that's ever happened to me in my life."

Well, two years later, in 1984, I'm at the NCAA Final Four with the University of Virginia basketball team. We get beat in the semifinals by the University of Houston in overtime, and the next night Georgetown is playing Houston for the National Championship. Now Freddie Brown is a senior point guard for Georgetown, and they upset Houston and win. When the game's over, John Thompson again makes a beeline to Brown and again gives him a bear hug, and it brought tears to my eyes. Everyone saw Thompson as this big, imposing, gruff man, but he proved he was a great coach because he had compassion and support and encouragement for a kid in the toughest moment of his life. That's what *real* toughness is. So, the question is, can you forgive *yourself* in the toughest moment of *your* life so you can let go of it and play your best the next time?

It's hard to say if heartbreak is in the mind, the heart, the soul, or the human spirit. You cannot take a picture of it. But we know it is there. It hurts, it can be devastating, and it might make you cry. It's okay if you *do* cry. I constantly tell people, "You'll have to go through the fire." It'd be as if you took a piece of raw metal out of the ground and put it into a hot furnace that burns away all the impurities and turns that piece of metal into a strengthened block of steel. You cannot become strong and special without going through the fire. It just never happens. It is part of your job to cherish it and to embrace it and come out of it stronger. There is no sense dreading or fearing it because, as you will learn, in many ways it is a blessing in disguise—as long as you are stronger than the things that happen to you. But it will demand a calmness about you, somewhat of a stoic response, and a decision that

What I Learned from Jim Valvano

The year I started coaching lacrosse and going to grad school at the University of Connecticut, Jim Valvano started at UCONN as an assistant basketball coach. Valvano says his 1982–83 NC State team that won the National Championship taught him a lesson that he carried through his fight with cancer: "Hope that things can get better despite adversity," he said. "That team taught me persistence, the idea of never ever quitting, don't ever give up, don't ever stop fighting." He stated that his favorite quote was "Trees would tap-dance, elephants would drive the Indianapolis 500, and Orson Welles would skip breakfast, lunch, and dinner before North Carolina State figured out a way to win the NCAA basketball tournament. This team taught me that elephants are going to be driving in the Indianapolis 500 someday."

the experience not only will not destroy you, but will make you better and stronger for having faced it.

You are not going to grow stronger from a heartbreaking loss—say, a day when you fall apart coming down the stretch with a chance to win or miss an easy putt on the last hole—if you ignore it or pretend it didn't happen. You only improve and get stronger if you respond to it in the right way. In the short run, it is helpful to talk about it or at least reflect on it yourself. Some people like to write about it. This way you can admit what you did wrong and learn from it. You figure out the correct thing to do in the situation mentally and emotionally. You have to learn from it. Then you can bounce back from it and embrace the situation the next time you're in it. It is not a tragedy unless you don't address what you did wrong and never learn from it. You have to ask yourself, "Did I panic? Did I get careful? Did I start guiding and steering? Did I get ahead of myself? Did I overreact and get negative and beat myself up? Did I start worrying about losing or messing up, or did I get ahead of myself and start thinking of what winning would mean to me before finishing the round?" The next step is deciding what you will do when faced with a similar situation.

Stay in the Moment, Even When You Practice

You should strive to stay focused in the moment on whatever your purpose is when you're in your practice session. Your overall goal ought to be attempting to get better each and every day when you practice. And trusting that if you do that, your career or your ultimate goal will take care of itself.

If you learn from it by being honest with yourself, you will be prepared for the next time you are in a similar situation. You will be inoculated, so to speak, and you will be ready to perform in situations you could not have handled if earlier you had not fallen on your face. It is all part of the journey. It is the beauty of sport. You have to handle the good and the bad, the joy and the agony. If you learn to make it through the fire, it will only make you stronger.

Take the example of Shane Lowry, who lost the 2016 US Open at Oakmont after carrying a four-shot lead into the final round. Dustin Johnson came on strong over the last eighteen holes to win, but Lowry's putter let him down on the back nine and he fell out of contention. It could have been a devastating loss and could have defined him, if he had allowed that to happen. But he didn't. Three years later, after winning in grand style at Portrush, he was the British Open champion. He told *Golf Digest* that he was able to put his collapse at Oakmont into perspective. "Dustin played some great golf and won. I had three three-putts in a row on 14, 15, 16. But it's behind me." Lowry also was clear and candid about his approach going into the final round of the British Open that he won: "The aim is to make the results not matter, even if they do. I'm competitive. I want to do as well as I can. But I still want to get to a place where hitting a 7-iron in the water is not the biggest deal in the world." Lowry learned from his Oakmont experience: "The one thing I took away [from Oakmont] is that I didn't play aggressively enough in the final round. So, without getting ahead of myself, I knew that if I made four or five birdies [at Portrush], I would be very hard to beat. I ended up making four." You see, you must do what Lowry did—honestly assess your setback and learn from it.

There might be nothing more satisfying than bouncing back after a poor performance. Nothing will impress others more than those who get good at doing that, and nothing will tell you more about your character and what you're all about. You can never change parts of your story, but you can definitely change *you* and how you *respond*. And you can make your life story more inspiring.

When you're going through a tough patch, it is decision time. Will it ruin your career? Will you give up on your dreams? Will you start doubting your ability? Or will you dig down deep and grow stronger? Instead of feeling sorry for yourself and wondering why this is happening to you, get honest and go to the history books and realize that every great athlete and golfer has gone through struggle and tough times, but all got past it and thrived.

Many players we have never heard of were destroyed by how they perceived their adversity and how they responded to it. If you want to be great, you can't do that. The great ones renew their commitment, renew their passion, and constantly renew their belief that some way, someday, it's going to fall in place and happen. This is just another way to separate yourself from others who couldn't deal with it or handle it. The more difficult and longer the struggle, the more the great ones loved

Words to Live By

A quote you commonly hear in the world of sport teams applies particularly to golf: "Nothing given, everything earned." It's a model for many teams. In other words, you only get what you earned, and you only deserve what you get. I like to use this little phrase to remind the players I talk to that they should never stop working hard, especially when they start feeling sorry for themselves or feel they aren't achieving success fast enough.

it, because it made a strong statement as to what they were all about. It is a wonderful skill to see: looking at heartbreak as a blessing, and as powerful and magical. You must believe it can be learned, and you must be willing to work hard at developing it. It is an opportunity to prove yourself. You wanted greatness to be hard, you wanted to be tested, you love that many others did not bounce back from heartbreak as you will. You are prepared for any test thrown your way. You know that you will respond with conviction. You will stay cool and calm. You know you can handle it. You will *choose* to embrace it.

You will train yourself to control what you can control—your response—and not try to control things you cannot control—stuff that happens to you. This is gut-check time.

Time to find out what you are all about and if you really want it. This is when you determine your destiny. You must decide that success is not about luck and what you're born with, but about what you do with what you've got and how you see and respond to the tough times you face. It is largely about how you bounce back from these experiences.

Yes, some of success is about staying hungry and disciplined when everything is coming easy and going your way, but most can handle *that*. Handling adversity is a big separator in the world of competition. Becoming mentally tough and resilient gives you a feeling of strength, of power, of being in control of yourself and your career. It makes you special and different. But you must learn to stay calm and coolheaded when others would be an emotional mess and fall apart. You might need the emotional maturity of a thirty-five-year-old at eighteen, but it

Love the Bad

Golf is a game of adversity. Yes, you have to go through the fire, but if you want to be a great golfer, you also have to love the bad, you have to expect the bad, just as you have to love the good and expect the good. It's all part of chasing your destiny.

is a part of being exceptional. You must be unflappable, regardless of what you face. You must be able to weather the storm.

By doing this, you develop a reputation for being a composed, mature competitor. You are like a rock or still water. You're unshakable and your opponents know it. And more important, *you* know it. Nothing surprises you. Nothing shakes or bothers you. You love doing things others choose not to do. You are always looking for ways to separate yourself. You do not want to be average or like everybody else. You have an inner resolve, a determination. Panic is not in your makeup. This is a big part of your edge. You had anticipated tough times and rough patches, and you are ready and prepared for anything and everything thrown at you. You know how you will respond to it. You will not let emotions rule. You will keep everything in perspective and respond like a seasoned veteran who knows how to play.

You will go through slumps, you will miss shots, you will miss easy putts, you will go through tough times. But this is part of why you love golf. It is hard, and most can't handle it. But you can, and you love that you are tough enough to do so. There might have been a time in your life when you could not handle the disappointment of the game. You overreacted and got lost in self-pity. You got negative. You got too emotional. You got into doubt and fear, but not anymore. You used to get ahead of yourself, worrying about playing badly. But now you are past that. You have matured. You have emotionally grown up. You have learned that golf is just a game. But it is a hard game and a game of mistakes. You now realize it is much more about how you deal with bad days and how you respond to the game than it is about mastering the game. You are learning it is more about mastering yourself and your mind and your emotions. You have learned that becoming a great golfer is a journey. It is more of a marathon than a sprint. But you know sooner or later your day will come.

You have learned that you will follow a process that requires you to hang strong and keep believing, even when it is hard to do so. You have a plan, a purpose, and a dream. You will honor it every day with an upbeat, enthusiastic attitude until things work out and go your way. Nothing will deter you in your quest. You welcome all challenges and tough times the game throws at you. You will always bounce back stronger and more resilient. It is clear in your mind that your time will come, and you will appreciate it even more because it was such a challenge—and you passed the test.

CHAPTER 6

Believing in You and Your Game

I don't know why you're practicing so hard to finish second.

—Babe Didrikson Zaharias

She said this to her fellow LPGA players on the practice range before a tournament. She won eighty-two amateur and professional events, including ten professional majors.

It's hard to fathom that I'd be telling a young player—or anyone for that matter—the following, because it goes against the grain. But to achieve greatness in this day and age, you need to develop a self-assured manner, a supreme confidence, even a sense of what others might see as cockiness. If you're not comfortable with comporting yourself in such a way because you think you'll be perceived as obnoxious or conceited or insufferable, you need to at least develop an *inner arrogance.* Maybe you don't tell others how good you think you are, but you better believe it yourself. You have to have a feeling inside that you deserve it, that you are destined to do something fantastic. It is what you are born to do. You must create your own reality. Others might say you are delusional, but you might just be brilliant because in some ways delusional is simply seeing it in your mind before it happens in reality.

Patrick Reed was criticized for saying he was one of the Top 5 players in the world after winning his third PGA Tour event, at Doral in 2014. Though he was officially ranked No. 20, he believed he was much better, and he said it for everyone to hear. Less than two years later, he was a force to be reckoned with at the 2016 Ryder Cup, amassing a 3-0-1 record

Remain in Your Bubble

Most players do their best by staying in their own little bubble or their own little world and not caring about others and things that they can't control. I know this sounds boring, but it works well for most players most of the time. If you can be into leaderboards and what other players are doing all of the time or some of the time as well as other potentially distracting thoughts and you can still play great, go ahead and do it, but you better make sure that's the right approach for you. Ben Hogan was maybe the best at staying in his bubble, totally unaware of outside distractions.

and defeating Rory McIlroy 1-up in their classic singles duel. Eighteen months after that, Reed was donning the green jacket as the 2018 Masters champion, and another strong showing at the 2018 Ryder Cup earned him the nickname Captain America.

Similar to the way athletes in other sports are not afraid to trash-talk their opponents and speak highly about their own abilities, the days of golfers going about their business in silence are mostly gone. Arnold Palmer said his father, Deacon, told him never to brag on himself and to let his clubs do the talking. You never heard Jack Nicklaus describe his golf game with braggadocio, even though he had unbelievable confidence in himself and his ability. Privately he once told the Ohio State golf team, "You have to be a legend in your own mind before you can be a legend in time." Today's competitive environment is somewhat different. It's okay to strut your stuff. It's all right to show a little swagger. Brooks Koepka, for example, said publicly during the week of the US Open at Shinnecock, "I know one thing: I'm the most confident player in this tournament." He won his second straight Open that week and has now captured four majors in three years and walks the fairways as if he owns them. Tiger Woods, early in his career, was probably the most outwardly confident player, telling the world that he was chasing Nicklaus's record of winning eighteen major championships.

It's not easy to believe in yourself, and to maintain that belief, no matter what. Everybody has ups and downs, and it's common to get derailed and lose your confidence, your self-belief, especially when you see other players doing better than you and making great use of their talent. It's like when I was teaching a large lecture class at the University of Virginia and I would tell the students, "Remember the day you got accepted here? You thought you were a genius and could do anything you put your mind to. But by the end of your second year, after seeing so many other really talented students around you, you're saying to yourself, 'I'm not as good as I thought I was. Maybe I can't do anything I put my mind to doing.'" That's a mistake that many people make. Over their lifetime they either convinced themselves or let "experts" convince them that they didn't have much potential. The minute you question your potential, you've just given yourself the greatest cop-out and excuse that is sure to end your commitment. You're done. You set up a self-fulfilling prophecy that controls your golf game. You need to love *your* talents and *your* potential because you will take it with you to the golf course every time you play. The biggest mistake you can make is to waste your time and energy lusting for talents that others possess. Your job is to believe and love the talents you *do* possess. Gary Player, because of his diminutive size, could have given up on believing in himself and his goals, but he used his mind to supersede what others perceived as a physical drawback. "If you are good enough, you are big enough," he has said.

Coaches and athletes in other sports understand the incredible importance for success of having an extremely high level of confidence. For example, I got a chance to go to one of the

Stay Unemotional

Treat each shot as separate and distinct. Make sure that you're not caring about any feelings regarding the last shot or any previous shots. The easiest way to do that is to not give any emotions to your shots.

birthday parties for Muhammad Ali when he turned seventy. They had parties in Scottsdale, Las Vegas, and Louisville, and I was invited to the one in Scottsdale. Ali could hardly walk. He needed help and couldn't talk much beyond a whisper, but he could understand everything. Tony Hawk, Mia Hamm, Johnny Bench, and Joe Morgan were all there, as well as some other great athletes. Everyone stood up and talked about the same thing. They wanted to thank Muhammad Ali for giving them permission to totally and completely believe in themselves, and they all talked about how much he influenced their lives.

During his prime, and even before that, Ali wasn't afraid to tell everyone else how good he was, and he acted as if he truly believed it. When Ali was asked once about playing golf, he responded, "I am the best, I just haven't played yet." That pretty well sums up his self-belief. As he said repeatedly, "Skill is not as important as will." It is one thing to love and admire Ali, but the important thing for your golf game is to learn from him.

Let's talk about *you* and how you feel about *yourself, your* ability, and *your* potential. What if, in another sport, at the beginning of a season a coach told you and your team it could come in fifth or sixth that year? How exciting would that be for you? What if that coach said the other guys in your area are a lot better than you are? Most likely, it would not make you feel great or inspire you. But what is much worse is to think this way of yourself. You cannot wait until you are winning and shooting low numbers before you believe. You must believe first. You need to believe in yourself unconditionally. For most, you must see it in your mind long before it actually happens. You must repeatedly rehearse these images. Your responsibility is to create a déjà vu experience so that you are comfortable when the moment happens. Numerous athletes in other sports have excelled by convincing themselves they were better than everyone else. By observing them and listening to their words, you can learn from them and create a belief in yourself and your dreams. It starts with telling yourself that you have faith in your ability, but how do you really believe it? In golf, as in other sports, the real heroics take place when no one else is watching. If you want to see how great you can be, your belief in your dreams must match your day-to-day commitment to making those dreams a reality. Too many golfers are highly committed to the physical aspects of their sport, but never the belief. You have to have both.

Michael Jordan is a great example. If Jordan had listened to his junior high school coach, who cut him from the team, he never would have gotten to the University of North Carolina, never would have won an NCAA championship, never would have gone on to the Chicago Bulls, never would have won six NBA championships, and never would have been one of the most dominant players in the game's history. The world is full of stories of people who were told they would never make it or wouldn't amount to anything, yet they believed in themselves unequivocally, worked unbelievably hard, and achieved incredible things. It's like the song you might have heard on the radio by the popular female singer Code Yellow: "You're Never Gonna Make Me Feel Bad about Myself." It describes

Leaderboards: To Look or Not to Look, That Is the Question

A few years ago, one of the commentators, who shall remain nameless, said if you do not dare look at leaderboards, you need to look for another career. And I said, well, I want you to just go out and execute your game plan that gives you your best chance. And I said, Bill Walsh, the legendary coach at Stanford and the San Francisco 49ers, wrote a book titled *The Score Takes Care of Itself.* Lombardi and John Wooden were all about just executing your game plan and keeping your emotions and your knee-jerk reactions out of your game, and trusting you will win if you execute your plan. It allows you to have single-minded attention to your stuff and to avoid the distractions of paying attention to what others are doing. I'll admit that looking at leaderboards sounds more exciting and makes you feel like more of a competitor, and it sounds macho. But unless you've won a lot recently, it usually doesn't help most people. Everything I teach is to stop worrying about others and stop constantly comparing yourself to others. Learn to live to *your* standards and chasing *your* potential.

the kind of self-belief that's necessary in today's world. Don't let others doubt your ability and define you.

There are also examples of a mentor showing such belief in a protégé that the student rose to unbelievable success. The boxing coach Constantine "Cus" D'Amato made Mike Tyson into one of the most feared boxers in history. Tyson grew up in a horrible family environment—his mother was a prostitute and his father was a pimp. As a kid, Tyson was arrested thirty-eight times. Finally, he was sent to a reform school, where someone introduced him to D'Amato. "The first time Cus watched me attempt to box, he told me I was going to be a heavyweight champion," Tyson has said. "I slowly went from a kid without any hope for my future to starting to believe I could be a world champion. Cus sold me on a new idea for my life and helped me to start to feel confident." D'Amato commented, "When I saw Mike, I saw a spark. I fanned the spark, and the spark became a flame. I fed the flame, and the flame became a fire. I fed the fire, and the fire became a raging blaze. That's what I did to turn Mike Tyson from a novice fighter into the heavyweight champion of the world." Find somebody to do this for *you*, and if necessary, constantly plant seeds into your own head and do it for yourself. Tyson, who has transformed his life from drugs and alcohol and a lack of respect for women, went on to say, "As I grew older, I've learned to have gratitude for those who have helped me so much."

This is what Harvey Penick did for great golfers such as Tom Kite, Ben Crenshaw, Kathy Whitworth, and Mickey Wright. It's what Jack Grout did for Jack Nicklaus, Mike Thomas did for his son Justin, Byron Nelson did for Tom Watson, Davis Love Jr. did for his son Davis III. It's also what Mike Furyk did for his son Jim. The story has been repeated many times.

You need to make your perception your reality, which Jim Furyk has done. He sees his swing as beautiful, and in his mind it looks like Adam Scott's swing—in other words, textbook perfect. All have to find their own way and their own swing that works for them. It's more about getting the ball to do what you want it to do, rather than how your swing looks. If the ball's going where you intend it to consistently, then it's a good swing. If you can start the ball on the line you want and turn it the way you want and on the trajectory you desire, that's way more important than how your swing looks. Beauty is in the eye of the beholder. It's clear to me that Furyk doesn't care what others think about his swing or how it looks on camera. He likes it and that's what matters. The same can be said of the top two finishers in the 2020 US Open at Winged Foot. Bryson DeChambeau (with his rigid left arm, clubs the same length, analytical approach, and massive power game) and Matt Wolff (with his unique hip kick-start, severe outside-to-inside loop, and nonmechanical manner) could not have two more contrasting styles, but each works for them. You have to have a lot of confidence in yourself to go out on tour with an unconventional game, but it seems that the best drivers of the ball often have the weirdest swings.

Part of believing in yourself is loving your unique personality. Back in the sixties and seventies we had Arnold Palmer, Jack Nicklaus, Gary Player, Lee Trevino, and Chi Chi Rodriguez, each with a uniquely different swing. I believe they loved that their swing was different from everybody else's because it made a statement about them and made them recognizable. In today's game, Dustin Johnson, Rickie Fowler, Justin Thomas, Matt Wolff, Bryson DeChambeau, Hideki Matsuyama, and Rory McIlroy all have individual styles and idiosyncrasies, yet all are immensely successful. You have to get good at not blaming your attitude flaws on your natural personality and wishing you were someone else or had someone else's personality.

I'm big on getting people to play within their personalities and learning to be themselves out in the competitive

When McIlroy Got a Tougher Attitude

On the eve of winning the 2011 US Open at Congressional, and after he fell apart in the final round of the Masters, Rory McIlroy told the media, "I decided I need to change my demeanor in future similar situations. I said I needed to be a little cocky, a little more arrogant on the golf course, and think a little bit more about myself, which I have tried to incorporate into my game. But just on the golf course. I have no desire to change my personality. I just try to have a bit of an attitude, you know? When I get myself into these positions, I have to really make sure I don't get ahead of myself. That's really the main thing. Even if I get four, five, six, seven ahead, I must try to get eight or ten ahead. I know probably more than anybody else what can happen if I don't, so I've got to stay focused on me and my game and what I can do when in control and go ahead and finish this thing off. It's about focusing on what I can do, and not worrying about the other players and what they are doing."

arena. You'll never believe in your ability if you are trying to be someone else. A lot of research has been done on the personality of great performers, and no legitimate researcher has ever determined that great performers have a single personality type—other than having enough guts and courage to be themselves and do it *their* way. Some are extroverted, such as Lee Trevino, who talked incessantly on the golf course. Some are introverted, such as Ben Hogan, who spoke to virtually no one during competition. Yet, they were both great champions. Today, the same can be said for Jordan Spieth, who usually has a running dialogue going with his caddie before and after he hits a shot, and Brooks Koepka, who comes across as somewhat stoic, almost in a bubble, on the course. These players don't ever try to be each other. They stay within their personalities and have cultivated a strong sense of inner confidence.

Greatness is a calling, and a choice. It's not something that you're just born with. If you find someone who seems to have

The Danger of Striving for Perfection

There is a big difference between always going back and working on your fundamentals versus continually making swing changes. It's an important distinction. For tour players, if they play in three or four tournaments in a row, their fundamentals often get lost. The same is true for amateurs who play a lot of competitive golf. Jack Nicklaus, if he got lost with his swing, would always go back to his fundamentals—grip, ball position, alignment, etc. For many players, if they get lost, instead of getting back to their fundamentals, they start looking for new swing information. They need to understand that they just have to reestablish *their* fundamentals. The first thing is to learn how to hit the ball, but once you know how to do that and are able to repeat it, then it ought to be about going back to your fundamentals. Always trying something different, constantly searching for perfection, can be a recipe for getting screwed up with your swing. That's why it's usually a good idea to stick with your same teacher, who will get you back to your fundamentals instead of giving you something different to try.

been born great, you need to say, "Well, that's good for that person, but it's not going to work for me." Greatness does not just happen. You have to want it, thirst for it, hunger for it, study it, fight for it, and want nothing else as badly as you pursue it. You also need to surround yourself with those who are excited by it and believe in your quest, whether that is a golf instructor, a coach, a sport psychologist, a caddie, a physical trainer, a spouse, or a close friend. Your support system needs to be behind you 100 percent. If not, find someone else who will back you all the way, no matter what.

Either think about playing great, or don't think about your golf game. Especially after a poor round, you must program your brain for what you want, not for what you don't want. Be sure to spend way more time reliving all the good shots and putts that you made that day and a lot less time replaying mistakes, if you do it at all. Take the negative emotions out of your mistakes and bad shots and just accept them. And stop taking your great shots and putts for granted. Attach strong, positive emotions and feelings to these shots. Strong emotions play a powerful role in which experiences you remember.

Worrying is the same as physically practicing wrong—if you do it a lot. A little bit of worry is fine if you're using it to prepare for your next tournament. But if you do all your preparation well, and then right before the tournament you quadruple the amount of worry, that's not going to produce the results you are looking for. I'd rather you worry early, using it to guide your practice and preparation, so as you near the competition, you don't have to worry, and you can have peace of mind that you're ready.

It's like the attitude the new sensation on tour, Will Zalatoris, brings to the course every time he tees it up. When he was on the Korn Ferry Tour, he averaged 80 percent of his greens hit in regulation. He also tied for 6th in his first US Open, at Winged Foot in 2020, and came within a stroke of winning the Masters in 2021 in his rookie appearance. When Will was six years old, he met Ken Venturi on a practice range. Venturi helped him with his grip, then sensing that Will had an intrinsic love for golf and a strong self-belief, he told his parents that their job was to stay out of the way.

Everyone has moments of doubt. But you have to be strong and persevere through them. You cannot get lost in doubt. You don't need to think that you have to have a perfect attitude when a great attitude will do just fine. I tell people if 90 percent of the time you have a great attitude, you've got it. One way to overcome doubt is to make sure you don't get mired in the pressure of competing. When Chicago Cubs manager Joe Maddon was guiding his 2016 team to their World Series championship (the first for the Cubs since 1908), he told them, "Do not let the pressure exceed the pleasure." In other words, make sure

The first time I worked with Tom Kite, we were at Doral with Gary Koch and Roger Maltbie. I read them a passage from Ben Hogan's all-time bestselling golf book, *Five Lessons: The Modern Fundamentals of Golf*, written with Herbert Warren Wind. When I finished reading it, Tom said, "That cannot be in that book."

I said, "No, it's on page 95."

"I've read that book two hundred times. I don't ever remember seeing that."

"When you read that book, you were looking for a way to perfect your swing. You weren't looking for what Hogan was trying to tell you on that page."

Here is what it said: "Most golfers acquire confidence over a period of time. Hogan had great confidence and a great swing. He played with a coolness and confidence that was even a marvel to the Scots, who coined the phrase 'The Wee Icemon.' Of the two—the swing and the confidence—he attained the swing first. Even after he had a swing that would win tournaments, he still had periods of uncertainty. He describes how it happened: 'I never felt genuinely confident about my game until 1946. Up to that year, while I knew once I was on the course and playing well that I had the stuff that day and would make a good showing, before a round I had no idea whether I'd be 69 or 79. I felt my game might go sour on any given morning. I had no assurance if I was a little off my best form that I could still produce a respectable round. My friends on the tour used to tell me I was silly to worry, that I had a grooved swing . . . but my self-doubting never stopped. Regardless of how well I was going, I was still concerned about the next day and the next.

"'In 1946 my attitude suddenly changed. I honestly began to feel that I could count on playing fairly well each time I went out, that there was no practical reason for me to feel I might suddenly lose it all. I guess what lay behind my new confidence was this: I had stopped trying to do a great many things perfectly, because it had become clear in my mind that this ambitious over-thoroughness, my perfectionism, was neither possible nor advisable, or even necessary. All you needed to groove were the fundamental movements—and there weren't so many of them. . . . I don't know what came first, the chicken or the egg, but at about the same time I began to feel that I had the stuff to play credible golf. *Even* when I was not at my best, my shotmaking started to take on a new and more stable consistency.'"

We can all learn from that.

that playing competitive golf is something you do because you *love* it. Make sure you enjoy the process, the experience, and the journey. Outcome is important, but do not let it own you to the point you are not able to perform.

Some players are always looking for a way to get better and better, and they work harder and harder, and to some degree that can be good. But it can be a dilemma for certain players who are never satisfied. Perfectionism can be a detriment. It's not easy to want more and at the same time be patient. I tell these players that it's okay to not be satisfied in their practice, but when they step on the golf course, they have to be satisfied with what they have, accept it, and go. I tell them to compartmentalize. An attitude of always wanting more is great when you're preparing and practicing, but when it's time to play, you have to be able to make an honest and accurate assessment of where your game is and what you're doing well at that moment and go play with it.

Some teachers are always telling their students that they've got to improve their swing. I think this often leads to an endless search for a perfection that doesn't exist and leads players to jumping around to different teachers, bouncing from one to the next and then getting confused by different teaching philosophies and approaches. History shows us that the truly great players usually had one or maybe two teachers, and they stuck with them for life. Rory McIlroy still sees mainly his childhood teacher, Michael Bannon, from Northern Ireland. Nicklaus worked only with Jack Grout until Grout passed away, then primarily with Jim Flick, until he passed away. Arnold Palmer listened only to his father, Deacon, and nobody else. Bobby Jones's only teacher was Stewart Maiden. Hall of Famer Nancy Lopez listened only to her father, Domingo. Rafael Alarcón taught Lorena Ochoa in Guadalajara from the time she was a little girl until she retired from competitive golf at age twenty-eight.

One could argue Tiger Woods was an exception. While it's true he has worked with several teachers, his first instructors, Rudy Duran and John Anselmo, not to mention his father, Earl, gave him an incredible foundation for the others to build on. Whether it was Butch Harmon, Hank Haney, Sean Foley, or Chris Como, Tiger's teachers always believed in him. It's also important that Tiger knew how to score by the time he was five years old. He could almost always get the ball in the hole regardless of how he was swinging, and he knew it. That knowledge freed him up. That's one thing you should learn from Tiger. If you're hitting about thirteen greens per round, that's about as good as it's going to get. It's not about perfecting your swing. It's about developing a swing you can compete with and learn to trust. Ultimately, it will be about you believing in *you* and your ability to get the ball in the hole.

Whatever you do, when you are struggling to find your swing, you must learn not to panic. Panic brings out all kinds of problems. If you start getting in trouble with your game, before you start searching for a new teacher or scanning the internet for advice, go back to what you were doing the last time you were playing well. I recently worked with a young player who wanted to try some different teachers, and I asked him, "When was the last time you played great?" He said 2017. So I asked him what he was doing in 2017. He went back to the notes he had written on his cell phone and looked at some video from then. He called me, all excited, and said, "Oh my God, my swing was so different then." I encouraged him to get together with his teacher, and they both agreed that he needed to go back to what he had been doing three years earlier. He told his teacher not to ever let him get this far off again. Sometimes, it's that simple.

The great European teacher Bob Torrance, who coached Padraig Harrington to three major championships and Bob's son, Sam, to the Ryder Cup captaincy, said it's one thing to be able to hit a great shot under pressure when you are feeling good, but it is a bigger thing to be able to hit a good shot under pressure when your swing isn't feeling so good. This is a real issue for a lot of average golfers as well as for professionals. It comes down to belief in your ability and knowing that you are able to get the ball in the hole and shoot a score, even if you don't have your best swing going that day. It's knowing that you know how to play golf, and it is about confidence in *you*, rather than confidence in your swing. I call this having *golf confidence* versus *swing confidence*. A lot of teachers will talk about having swing confidence, but ultimately it comes down to having golf confidence—your belief in yourself and your ability to get the ball in the hole. A lot of tour players can only score when their swing is where they want it. They play really good golf about four times a year. But the great players have golf confidence—or self-confidence—in their ability to score, regardless of how they're hitting it. They just change their strategy, and they see it as fun and a source of pride to find a way to get the ball in the hole on days when they're not hitting it great. Bryson DeChambeau is a good example. People forget that before he won the US Open, he had already won the US Amateur and the NCAA Championship. Before he decided to change his body makeup and turn his game into a power game, he already had a strong belief in himself, in his ability to score, and in his ability to handle pressure at the highest level.

Phil Kept Believing

People often think of Phil Mickelson as always possessing incredible talent and confidence because he was a top collegiate player, won the US Amateur, and even captured a tour event before turning professional. But they forget that Lefty played in forty-seven major championships before he won his first one, the 2004 Masters. He had multiple close calls and resulting disappointments—even frustrating finishes, such as in numerous US Opens, where he has finished second six times! But since he won that first major championship at Augusta, he has won two more Masters, two PGA Championships, and a British Open. He believed in himself and what he was doing for more than thirteen years before breaking through with that first professional major victory. His self-belief and hard work paid off again in his epic win at the 2021 PGA, as he became the oldest major champion in history at age fifty. It's a good thing he didn't give up too early or stop trying too soon or *stop believing in himself!* He never would have fulfilled his dream.

Often, you have to downplay the situation and find a way to get the ball in the hole with what you have on that day. It's what Tiger Woods was trying to tell the world when he said he was winning with his C game. Other times, it is about making the other competitors disappear in your mind and just playing against yourself and the golf course, lost in your own little world. It's like when Elina Svitolina, from Ukraine, defeated Serena Williams in the 2016 Olympics. Svitolina said, "I just relaxed and went for my shots. I stayed in the moment and played the ball. I did not play Serena, I simply looked for the ball and played the ball."

If you have a strong mind, you can talk yourself into believing you will do great things. After Tiger holed a testing, left-to-right six-footer to tie Bob May on the 72nd hole at the 2000 PGA at Valhalla, Steve Williams, his caddie, asked him what he was thinking over the putt. Tiger said, "My mom can hole that putt. I'm Tiger Woods. Of course I will hole it." He went on to win the three-hole playoff with May and capture his third straight major championship of the so-called Tiger Slam.

Now, *that's* believing in your ability. *That's* the kind of self-belief I want you to have. You can create that kind of confidence. But it doesn't come easy, and it will take a lot of discipline, mental work, and physical practice.

CHAPTER 7

A Quiet Mind Will Set
Your Talent Free

You must feel tranquil and at peace. I have never
been troubled by nerves in golf because I felt I had
nothing to lose and everything to gain when I played.

—Harry Vardon, winner of six British
Opens, more than any other player

The quote above is from one of the most dominant golfers
in the history of the game. Harry Vardon was so influential
in the UK and the United States from about 1896 to 1920 that
the basic grip most golfers use today is named after him—it's
the way he held the club. Because he consistently scored lower
than the other players of his generation, the PGA Tour branded
its annual award for the lowest stroke average the Vardon Trophy. Vardon is considered to have had an almost-perfect swing
technically. But many do not realize that what allowed him
to get the ball in the hole so efficiently, win all those championships (he also won a US Open), and be so dominant on

the golf course was his quiet mind and ability to let go when playing the game. More than 100 years ago, Vardon knew that it doesn't matter how good your swing is. If you don't trust it on the golf course and play with an unconscious mindset, you'll never reach your potential. He understood that a quiet mind is necessary to achieving greatness in golf.

Vardon got a quiet mind by convincing himself he had nothing to lose and everything to gain—a great way to deflect pressure. There are many ways to do this. You can downplay the importance by telling yourself something like *This shot doesn't matter. This round doesn't matter. I'm going to play hundreds of rounds in my life. I've done this many times before.* But be assured that going to the golf course thinking in ways that put pressure on you will tend to activate your thinking and turn on

Always, One Shot at a Time

Never forget the importance of taking it one shot at a time. And taking every shot as it comes, accepting it, never getting flustered, and just going to the next shot. You have to get good at doing that. Once a shot is over, never dwell on it. You cannot hit it again. It's time to move on and concentrate on making your next shot your best shot.

your conscious mind. You don't want to be careless, but there is a benefit in caring less.

To excel at this game, you must be able to turn off your conscious, analytical mind when it's time to execute a shot, whether it's a full swing, a pitch, a chip, a bunker shot, or a putt. This is what I mean when I say *I want you to think like an athlete*. I want you to *react* to the shot you are about to play without conscious thought. I want you to have a feeling of giving up control. That might seem counterintuitive—and even scary—for many people, but if you can train yourself to do that, you will hit the shots of your dreams. If you're thinking mechanically when it's time to move your body to swing, pitch, or putt, then you're thinking like an intermediate-level athlete. I want you to think like an advanced athlete—unconsciously.

I like to say, "There's a time to train, and there's a time to trust." That's an athletic way of looking at it. The bottom line is, in target-oriented sports, and especially in golf, you have to get to the point where your mind is *out there, into the target*. Now, we can have a long and great discussion about what a "target orientation" is. But for now, just know that it's out there where you want the ball to go. Your vision could be a target, such as the pin on the green or a branch on a distant tree. It could be a ball flight. It could be a dotted line. It could be anything you want it to be, but whatever it is, it has to be *out there* and it has to be consistent with where you want the ball to go.

It is easy to guide and steer to a small target, and it is easy to let go to a big target. But you must train your mind to let go to a smaller target to become an advanced golfer, to be your best. A lot of players tell me when they're faced with a wide fairway or they're hitting into a lake when practicing, they hit the ball dead straight. It's because they are able to relax. They let it go and free up their swing. So you need to have the sensation that you are swinging freely, but do it to a small target. It's like when SpaceX is sending astronauts to the International Space Station: they can't simply shoot the rocket up into nothing and hope the capsule will find the target. You need to be target-oriented with your golf swing, but then let it go freely.

In educational psychology, there has been a lot of research over the years regarding right-brain and left-brain thinking. The research suggests that the left brain is responsible for analytical thought, such as solving a math problem or figuring out a chemistry equation or computing the amount of thrust in a jet engine. In golf, you would use your left brain to develop the mechanical parts of your swing or putting stroke, or determine your yardage to the hole or assess the wind conditions or your strategy before you step up to the ball to swing, pitch, or putt.

The right brain is responsible for creativity, emotions, imagination, feelings, and so forth, such as freedom of expression in art or music or dance or sport. It's what is sometimes referred to as getting in the flow. In golf, this would include visualizing a shot, sensing the break on a putt, reacting to your target, or swinging the club without conscious thought.

What Nicklaus Said to Jacklin Before "the Concession"

Tony Jacklin, recounting his great final match with Jack Nicklaus in the 1969 Ryder Cup at Royal Birkdale noted that the pressure was unbelievable coming down the 18th fairway. The two players were deadlocked in the final match, and the overall team score was tied. Jacklin said, "As I'm hurrying off the 18th tee, eager to get to my ball ahead of Jack, he hollered after me, 'Tony,' so I waited as he caught up to me. He put his arm around my shoulder and said, 'Are you nervous?' 'Jack, I'm bloody petrified,' I said. Jack said, 'Well, if it's any consolation, I feel the same way.' And it put it all in perspective."

I want you to learn to use your left brain when you are gathering information and learning, and your right brain when it's time to move your body and be athletic.

It's okay to think about your body some of the time when you're training and working on your technique. For example, it's okay to think about what your hands and arms are doing when you're trying to develop your golf swing. You're training your various muscles to make certain movements that become repeatable over time—perhaps an early wrist cock going back, or leading your downswing with your lower body, or establishing

> *You can't hit and think at the same time.*
>
> —Yogi Berra

better posture at address. But you do all that work in training so when you get on the golf course, you don't have to think about it. You can just trust it. If I owned the world of golf instruction, students would do all of their technical work in front of a mirror without a ball or a target, and that way they would never develop any bad mental habits. Some of the players who come to me have highly advanced technique, but they've never let go of thinking about it. I'll have them stand in front of a mirror in my basement. I ask them to look at themselves in the mirror while making golf swings because I want them to fall in love with their swing. Most of the time, they can't believe how good their swing looks. They realize they aren't doing any of the bad things they usually worry about. I want them to see that their swing is deserving of trust. So they can stop worrying about their mechanics. They can just let go, free up, and swing without conscious thought. Many golfers have constantly been told all the things that are wrong with their technique, so this becomes their image of their swing, even when it is really good.

A lot of people hit so many balls working on their swing that pretty soon it becomes a dominant habit. They become so accustomed to it that they continue to work on their swing on the course and *pretend* they're playing golf. As a result, they never actually *play* golf. They just go on the course day after day, work on their swing, and wonder why they are not playing better.

Most people who set out to learn how to play golf with instruction—finding a teacher, taking lessons, practicing drills—need to understand the three stages of competency: (1) unconsciously incompetent, (2) consciously competent, and (3) unconsciously competent.

If you're a new golfer, you're going to be unconscious about your swing or stroke, and you're going to be incompetent at it. You are *unconsciously incompetent* at that move.

How Would You Play If Someone's Life Depended on It?

Ask yourself, how would you play if you knew this would be the last tournament or last round you could ever play in? When I pose that question to my students, they all say, "Oh, I would play fearlessly. I'd really turn it loose! I would just play to play great. It would be my last shot at it." Similarly, what if your wife or your children were kidnapped and someone told you that you would never see them again unless you shot in the 60s for your next four rounds? My students always say, "Well, I promise you one thing, I wouldn't be worrying about my swing. I wouldn't care about my putting stroke. I'd just go out there and find a way to get the ball in the hole." Interestingly, I have heard many tour players say, "Get me into contention on the weekend, and that's what I do. I forget about my swing and just find a way to score as low as possible. But on Thursday and Friday, I'm out there thinking about my golf swing, trying to find my game, worrying about the greens, complaining about course conditions, concerned about the weather, not liking my pairing, frustrated at the pace of play. I'm distracted by all this superfluous stuff. But get me in contention and I become single-minded and don't care about anything but making a score." That's the mindset I'm talking about. I want you to have it all the time, in every round you play.

As you practice the move you are trying to make, you start becoming an intermediate performer, where you're consciously starting to develop competency. Now you're conscious about what you are doing, and it takes a lot of effort, so your muscles aren't as relaxed, and you won't have as much rhythm, flow, or speed as is ultimately desired. But you start to develop competency, and in this stage you are becoming *consciously competent.*

An advanced performer becomes *unconsciously competent.* This person can do the technique without having to think about it. It becomes second nature. It has a flow, and it's smooth. Whether you are throwing a baseball, playing a piece of music, or hitting a pitch shot, you do it without thinking about *how* you're doing it.

I usually point out to people that anytime you change teachers or change your approach to the golf swing or alter your putting technique, you go back to being an intermediate performer, who is consciously developing competency. With a lot of practice over time, you will become consciously competent again. These changes usually will take a while, even if they seem minor. So you better make sure you want to do this. That's where your dedication and perseverance come into play.

I often relate this to music instruction because the musicians I work with deal with the same kinds of issues as golfers do. Musicians are trying to play flawlessly, usually in a group with other musicians, and in front of an audience. A guitar player in a rock band, for example, will tell me he usually plays a lot better if he also has to sing, because he totally lets go of any conscious control over the guitar. Drummers will tell me the same thing. They'll say that even if they're not supposed to be singing at all, they'll *pretend* to be singing. It gets their mind off the drumming. Now, I could find a great jazz musician who learned totally by feel and by ear and never thought about reading music or how technically to play the instrument and who is unbelievably good. And just as we can find child prodigies in music, we can find them in golf. If you look at video of Tiger Woods or Rory McIlroy when they were five years old, their swings don't look a whole lot different from what they do today. The main difference is they are bigger and stronger. But the overall action is pretty much the same. In other words, certain people didn't have to go through these stages. They were

Prospective Tour Players: It's Easier to Shoot Low on Tour

I work with a player on the Korn Ferry Tour who routinely shoots 18 under par for a tournament. He never shot close to 18 under in college. It illustrates the point I always tell my young players, particularly kids in college, who are watching the scores on tour and see these unbelievable numbers, such as 20 under par to win the tournament. (Dustin Johnson shot 30 under at the 2020 Northern Trust!) In college you're probably not going to shoot 20 under par because they don't want you to shoot 20 under par. But when you turn pro, it's all about television ratings, and TV wants to see low scores. You don't have to *try* to shoot low scores.

The courses are set up to shoot low scores. It's all about whether you're going to let yourself shoot low scores. But if you go and look at Jordan Spieth, if you look at Justin Thomas, if you look at Matthew Wolff, if you look at Collin Morikawa, I promise you they're scoring average is lower playing professional golf than it was playing college golf. It's because the courses are set up that way. I'm just telling these young players that because I don't want them to be intimidated. I want them to have the attitude that it's just a number, don't give it any meaning. The course will give it to you if you execute. But when players turn pro, they think they've got to hit 5-irons at every pin, and they blow themselves out of the tournament. On tour, you have perfect greens, perfect bunkers, everything is uniform, which makes it much easier to score low.

playing unconsciously almost from the time they started, just by imitating others.

It's similar to someone who is self-conscious on the dance floor. Some people feel that they can't dance until they have a few drinks. When they're sober, they're thinking about how badly they dance, they are instructing their hands, their head, and their feet what to do, and they look as if they have no rhythm or flow. Get a few beers in them and all of a sudden they feel like Fred Astaire, and the next day their friend says, "Oh, man, you were dancing unbelievable last night." The person says, "Well, I can't dance." And the friend says, "Look at this video I took on my phone—you sure could dance last night." All that happened is they stopped instructing and just listened to the music and let their body react to it. In playing golf, we have to be in that state of flow drug-free.

It's like when you go to Disney World and an artist does a caricature of you or your kid. The artist just looks at your face and his hand responds to what he's looking at. He doesn't look at his hand and tell his hand what to do to draw the caricature. It just happens by instinct. After hours of practice, he's become unconsciously competent.

So artists have a picture in their mind and their body responds to it. Musicians hear a song in their head and their body responds to it. Golfers see the target with their eyes or in their mind's eye, and their body responds to it. That's where you want to go with your golf game.

Speaking of music, several tour players have over the years related that they had a certain song going through their head when they were playing well. Recently, Matthew Wolff, after a strong finish in a tournament, said, "I have to give credit to the ice cream truck. I just had that ice cream truck song going through my head all day today. It really helped me be unconscious." Back in the early 1970s, the tour player Jerry Heard relied on a popular song to allow him to go unconscious. In

What Do You See in the Mirror?

If you look in the mirror and you don't believe that you can do something or you don't like what you see, you have to learn to not believe what you see in the mirror, and you have to train yourself to see yourself in a different way. I tell a lot of players I work with that you have to learn to see yourself the way *I* see you—loaded with talent and potential. It's like in boxing: you can't hit what you can't see. Live your life as if everything were a miracle, or as if nothing were a miracle. We can talk about reality, but show me some magic.

1972, *Sports Illustrated* reported, "Off the course, [Heard] is a jittery fellow who seeks out any diversion to keep from thinking about the tournament at hand, or his own game. But then he changes. He calms down and whistles, usually 'Take Me Home, Country Roads,' strolling down the fairways." Jack Nicklaus has said that during one of his two US Amateur victories, he had a Carol Channing song going through his head. The point is, a catchy song or tune can get your conscious mind turned off and can help you go unconscious on the course.

Some people I work with say, "So you want me unconscious all the time on the course?" Well, I want you unconscious at least when it's time to move your body. It's okay to do some analytical thinking before then. There's a time and a place behind the ball or away from the ball to get your yardage, select your club, make up your mind, and commit to your decision. But then once your shot routine starts, you need to get into *playing* golf and being *athletic* (responding to the target). I like players to go with their first instinct because it keeps them from turning on their conscious mind while they're preparing to execute the shot. When it's time to move your body to hit a shot or make a pitch or a putting stroke, you have to be athletic with an unconscious mindset. Also, the more decisive you are—the more you tell yourself, *I'm not walking up to that ball until I've totally made up my mind*—the easier it's going to be to go unconscious. Even a little doubt or indecisiveness will tend to turn on your conscious mind and cause you to overcontrol your motion.

During the 2020 US Open at Winged Foot, we all got an up-close and personal look through the TV cameras at how

A big heart and a great mind are more important than technical perfection.

—Bob Torrance, legendary Scottish teacher, and father of Sam Torrance, Ryder Cup captain the eventual winner, Bryson DeChambeau, uses an incredible amount of analytical thinking and processing of information in preparation for each shot. A lot of TV analysts point out his scientific approach—studying his yardage book, discussing all the variables with his caddie, analyzing the situation, checking the wind, figuring out where to land the ball. However, what the analysts fail to mention is that once he runs all that input through his "computer"—his brain—and has all that information in place, he turns that part of his mind off, becomes unconscious, frees up, and turns it loose. He lets it rip off the tee and becomes target-oriented with his iron shots and even his putts.

You should develop a solid and complete game plan before a competitive round. By the time your practice round is over, I would like you to already know what target you're going to look at off every tee shot. I would like you to already know what club you're going to hit and what weather conditions would change it, so you don't have to do a lot of thinking when you get on the golf course. I would like you to already know, for example, which par 5s you are going for in two and at what distance, and when and where you are going to lay up.

In other words, I would like you to have your strategy already laid out for how you're going to play the golf course. Doing the preparation will help you to have a quiet mind while playing. It's like a basketball team early in the year when they're learning a new offense. Everyone's running around trying to remember where to go and what to do. But as the season goes on, it becomes all instinct, all automatic. Preparation is key. You don't have to think so much once you're competing. And you start to play better and better.

Some players go so far as letting their caddie just give them the yardage and tell them what club to hit. *You read the putts for me and tell me where to hit it.* The advantage of that is it limits the need to think. It's a lot like a pitcher letting the catcher call all the pitches and the locations for him. With other players, I tell them to go with their first instinct. If the caddie gives you the yardage, go with your initial thought on club selection. Go with your first look on green reading. Now, in between shots, you can either stay positive or you can totally

Have Only One Judge

The renowned ballet dancer Suzanne Farrell once told writer Joshua Wolf Shenk that she would only think of pleasing George Balanchine, her ultra-famous choreographer. "I would try my hardest to do what he wanted and dance well, and he would be the only judge, relieving me of having to criticize myself." I would love golfers to have that attitude with their swing teachers and their sport psychologists. Let them do the judging and critiquing. You just do.

let your mind wander. But when it's time to step up to the ball, you have to go unconscious. When I talk about a quiet mind, what I care about is, when it's time to move your body, I want your conscious mind turned off, and I want you target-oriented.

I've had people ask me, "Well, what if I've got to play a round of golf and I just can't do it without swing thoughts?" I tell them, "If I have to make a deal with the devil, I'll let you for a while have *one* swing thought, but it better be *effortless*. It better be *consistent*. It better fit into your *routine*. And it better *not change* every time you don't hit a great shot."

Golfers who are motivated tend to get overtaught technically with an overemphasis on technique. It's not that it's wrong. It's just that you had better not get lost in it. You have to remember that, ultimately, to get where you want to go as a golfer, you have to become unconsciously competent. That's why we practice. So we don't have to think about it when we play.

It always amazes me how golfers are willing to play consciously, day after day, no matter how poorly they perform. Yet, ask them to play unconsciously, and if they miss one shot, they want to run back to playing consciously. You must stick with playing unconsciously and being athletic long enough to get comfortable with it and to realize the benefits. For some, their mind is so busy and consciously active that every time they hit a shot that isn't perfect, they try a different swing thought that their teacher has given them or they made up themselves. Others are worse: they have been to numerous teachers, and

In Competition, Lock In

In other sports, coaches have a saying that once the game starts, *you have to lock in.* As soon as the competition begins, you cannot be thinking of anything other than the game and what you need to do to succeed. Executing your game plan is your sole focus. The same should be true of your golfing mindset. No distractions. No random thoughts. No negativity. From the time you step onto the first tee until you make your final putt on the last green, nothing matters except sticking to your routine and shooting the best score possible.

when they miss a shot, they try swing thoughts from different teachers. They do it day after day without satisfactory results, but never decide to go in a different direction. They are addicted to an active, conscious mind that has worked in many other activities they have been successful at. But it will never work with their golf game. At some point, a dramatic change to a quiet, unconscious mind is necessary to become a complete golfer. Preconceived notions and beliefs that don't work must be dumped. At first, doing so will feel scary, but with time it will get comfortable, and it will feel athletic and effortless. You will finally be *playing* golf.

It's like Jane Blalock once said about her routine before starting a competitive round: "I go into the locker room and find a corner by myself and just sit there. I try to achieve a peaceful state of nothingness that will carry over onto the golf course. If I get the feeling of quiet and obliviousness within myself, I feel I can't lose." Blalock won twenty-seven times on the LPGA Tour and still holds the record for most consecutive cuts made (299) on any professional tour!

To be great, you must open your mind to all possibilities and let go of all limits of what you might do if you get your mind right. Following that advice will help you reach your fullest potential. You need to understand that the reason for training is to become unconsciously competent with your golf swing and your short game. When you do that, you will develop a quiet mind that will set your talent free.

CHAPTER 8

How to Develop
Effective Routines

A routine is not a routine if you have to think about it.

—Davis Love Jr.

When most golfers hear the word *routine*, they usually think of a pre-shot routine. But there are other types of routines that you need to follow, not just the one right before you hit a shot. For example, there are also pre-practice routines, practice routines, pre-tournament-round routines, and post-round routines. While the world of sport has different kinds of routines, all of them are done with two overall objectives: to produce comfort and peace of mind.

Let's talk about pre-shot routines first. One of the most important steps to making your next shot your best shot is having a consistent and repeatable pre-shot routine. I'm talking about the sequence of thoughts and movements that you need to follow before you swing the club, execute a pitch or chip shot, or stroke a putt. You need to practice this routine until it becomes second nature, so you do it the same way every time. Especially in pressure situations, having a routine and sticking to it for every shot can keep you focused, eliminate doubt, maintain your rhythm, and help you stay calm.

A solid, consistent routine allows you to be clear and committed on every shot. I would like what you do behind the ball to be very routinized, what you do over the ball to become a consistent routine, and then after you hit your shot, I want you to accept it and go to your next shot so you can make *that* your best shot. It might sound like a challenge to create and execute a consistent routine shot after shot, but it's going to help you play better and better.

I read a lot about routines that I don't like. I think people tend to hear about being routinized and all of a sudden think they have to become a serious, uptight nerd with an unbelievably complicated, long, detailed checklist of items they need to go through before they pull the trigger. I want you to have a short, simple routine. Some players just copy a tour player whose routine they like and seems to fit their own personality. Other players create a routine that is unique to themselves and that they like. Whatever your routine is, it should be athletic and intuitive. I don't want it to be complicated, and I want you to spend very little time over the ball, especially between your last look at the target and the start of your backswing.

Routines are not just something you should do while playing the game. They should start in practice, even *ahead of* practice. So before you go to the golf course to a practice session, make it a routine to first have a plan for what you're going to do and for how long you're going to do it. Ask yourself, "What is my purpose in going to practice? What parts of my game am I going to work on today?" You need a planned routine. A football or basketball coach would never conduct a practice session without a sheet that has every fifteen minutes blocked out with a plan for what each of the players is going to work on, and the coach sticks to that plan. Is there some room for variation or adjustment? Yes. It doesn't have to be written down, but most great golfers have a plan when they go to the practice range. They don't just show up and say, "Hmmm, I wonder what I can do today?"

Let's get into more specifics regarding your practice-plan routine. Ask yourself, "Where is my game lately?" There's a time and a place to say, "Well, right now I need to spend more time on my long game." But sometimes you might say, "I also need to put some time into my short game, to at least keep it there." It's like the quote from the legendary teacher Harvey Penick, who taught both Ben Crenshaw and Tom Kite: "Don't forget how to putt when you start hitting it great like that."

You should have a plan for what you're doing every time you practice, and then you should have a plan for when you get closer to tournament time. A lot of people do what I call "panic practicing." They suddenly start changing everything the last day before a tournament because they're worried. Sometimes they overreact to one missed practice shot and lose faith in their swing. What they should do instead is say, "Okay, now I've

got to get more into my routine." I coach my players to finish
every practice session with forty minutes of hitting golf shots.
They are doing their pre-shot routine and hitting a high cut, a
high draw, a low cut, a low draw. They are hitting specific golf
shots to actual targets, and not hitting the same shot twice in
a row. As part of their routine, a lot of guys will start playing
the golf course in their mind before they even get there, if they
know the course at all. They might play entire rounds on the
range, hitting a driver, then a short or long iron, then a pitch,
then back to the driver. I like players to taper their practice as
they get near tournament time, like a swimmer doing fewer and
fewer laps to preserve stamina. Don't quadruple the amount of
practice the last three days before a tournament, an urge a lot
of players have based on panic rather than a plan. You would
never find a good football or basketball coach who suddenly has
five-hour practices the day or two before a game. Their practices
are efficient, and they get done what they want to get done,
but they're not going to overpractice right before a big game.

The night before a tournament round, players need to have
a routine for how many hours of sleep they're going to get.
Based on your tee time, determine what time you need to go
to bed. Because you play a sport that sometimes requires you
to get up early in the morning, make it part of your routine to
turn off the TV late at night. Factor into your routine how late
you eat or drink, as well as *what* you eat or drink, so it doesn't
bother your sleep. Before they fall asleep, I like players to take
fifteen or twenty minutes and turn off their phone, close the

You Must Have Some Non-negotiables

If you want to be great as a golfer, you need some non-negotiable attitudes and behaviors that you know are absolutely crucial to you, and you must not allow yourself to deviate from them.

For example:

- I will do my routine on every shot.
- I will be decisive and committed on every swing.
- I will be unflappable.
- I will play one shot at a time.

I encourage you to have some non-negotiables and tell yourself, "I'm not going to get where I want to go if I break these rules." You decide what they are, but you have to have standards that you live by and play by.

computer, eliminate any other distractions, and just visualize the next day's round. In your head, go through your mental processes, your attitude, and your game plan, reviewing your targets off tees and preparing your strategy for the next day.

You should have checked the weather forecast so you have already prepared your clothing for rain or cold or wind or high heat and how you will handle delays in play due to inclement weather. For example, know ahead of time what you're going to do if there's a ninety-minute thunderstorm delay. Are you going to talk to other players? Or stay to yourself? How long before it's time to go back onto the golf course are you going to start getting your mind back into golf? Other players might be flipping out because of the delay and then it throws off their rhythm, while you can use it to your advantage by staying calm, cool, and collected.

The night before, check your pairing so you know whether it's going to be someone easy to play with or someone who is difficult. You want to be prepared so there are no surprises, and you'll know how you're going to deal with it. As the Carly Simon song "Anticipation" illustrates, prepare to be ready mentally and emotionally for anything that might happen the next day. At night, prepare yourself for whatever might come your way. If something difficult or bizarre happens, you'll handle it well. If nothing happens, so be it. At least you weren't caught off guard. I am a big believer in anticipating anything and everything that could possibly happen at the golf course the next day, and then preparing how to respond to it and deal with it. It is an effective way of separating yourself from other players and gaining an edge.

If you're in a strange city, scout out the driving route the day before you play and factor in plenty of time to get from your hotel to the course, taking traffic into consideration. The purpose of overplanning is to eliminate panic and rushing. The day before your round, pre-determine how many hours before your tee time you will get up. For most tour players, it's probably somewhere between three or four hours. If you have a 7:00 a.m. tee time, which is not unusual on tour or in top amateur tournaments, you might have to get up at 3:30 or 4:00 in the morning. You might need to do a lot of stretching after your shower and eat well in advance so your body's systems are taken care of before you warm up. Most of the players I work with have a set time they want to arrive at the course, and they have a set time they want to get to the practice tee or short-game area. It varies from player to player. I have players who get to the range twenty-five minutes before their tee time; for others it's an hour and a half. I don't care how much time you take, but it should be consistent before every round. Also, it's a good idea to start to follow this routine three or four days before a tournament, either in practice rounds or at your home course. Routines are designed to put you in the right rhythm and give you comfort, so take advantage of that and get comfortable. It's the same reason airline pilots have a checklist they go through before every flight. They leave nothing to chance.

Most experienced players have an organized system. Do they putt first, then go to the range? Do they start with their short irons and work up to the driver? Tom Watson sometimes starts with his 4-iron because he says it helps to loosen him up and makes the other clubs seem easier to hit. Some players warm up with their even-numbered clubs one day and their odd-numbered clubs the next. After the driver, they usually finish by hitting some wedges and bunker shots. I like my players to "play" the first nine holes on the range, hitting a driver, then, say, 8-iron, etc. They play holes in this manner for the last twenty-five or thirty balls so they're already into their process and their pre-shot routine when they get to the first tee. On the putting green before a competitive round, they only do their putting routine, even to the point of marking their ball, sighting the line on their ball if that's what they do, and *using only one ball.* If they're at a tournament, they are not working on their stroke before a round. (They save that for after the round.) Most guys arrive at the tee three to five minutes before their tee time so they're never late.

Post-round, my only rule is, if you loved how you played, and you loved everything in your game, and you have peace of mind, then I don't mandate that you go to the practice area afterward. But if any part of your game is going to cause you to go back to dinner or your hotel room and lie in bed and worry, then you should go to the practice area and get it cleaned up. Get feeling good so when you leave the golf course, you can forget about golf until it's time that night to take your fifteen to twenty minutes of mental preparation for the next day before you fall asleep. If you *don't* go practice for a little bit and you're going to worry, then you're out of your routine. Some players don't want to put too much emphasis on one part of their game, so if they go to the range, they spend a little bit of time on everything. For example, Watson once told me that if he concentrated too much on one aspect of his game, say his pitching, the next time he played, the rest of his game didn't measure up. That's why he makes sure that after working hard on a certain area of his game he spends a little time taking care of everything else.

I've never seen a top player who didn't have a consistent pre-shot routine and a consistent routine before and after every competitive round. Stay committed to whatever routine you develop—keeping it simple and intuitive—and you'll be on your way to playing the best golf of your life.

CHAPTER 9

Using Statistics to Guide
Your Practice and Play

The only way to win tournaments is with the short game. Over half your shots out here are within thirty or forty yards of the green.

—Phil Mickelson

To continue on your quest to make your next shot your best shot, I think it's a good idea to *occasionally* keep track of various statistics after your rounds, so you can better understand your game and your tendencies. Simply use what you find out to guide your practice, make your time spent practicing more efficient and productive, give direction to your course-management strategies, and, ultimately, be the best golfer you can be.

I am not a statistics nut, and I don't want you to track all your rounds and each of your shots every time you play. I've seen too many times with tour players and good amateurs how an overemphasis on stats can become an obsession and ultimately be counterproductive. In every sport, including golf, it is common to win the stat contest and lose or get beaten. As I will elaborate later in this chapter, stats are better for predicting scoring average and consistency than winning. Winning has a lot more to do with *believing* you can win than it has to do with stats. Stats are important, but they are not more important than getting the ball in the hole and finding a way to win. For example, so many people talk about Tiger Woods being a great putter. But the truth is, Tiger putts better when he has a chance to win than he does on average. Jack Nicklaus almost always seemed to make a putt on the last hole or coming down the stretch when he needed it to win. A lot of winning is about making putts at the right time—when you really need them. It's hard to analyze that statistically. Also, another word of warning: This data that we get from stats is just a starting point that will help you and your teacher put a plan together for what you need to work on. It serves merely as a guide for how to spend your practice time and how to plan your course management. However, you need to make sure that your self-image changes as your skills change. When you study your stats, don't let them become your golfing identity. I've known golfers who used to be poor drivers and improved their driving tremendously, but then they went to play in a tournament and drove the ball badly because that's how they still saw themselves. Avoid that mistake. Don't make what you learn from stats into a death sentence. If you see that your putting stats aren't very good, for instance, you can't start seeing yourself as a terrible putter. Stats are just information about your game at the present moment, and you can use them wisely to help you improve in the future. But you must constantly bring your mind up to the level of your new skills, or your new skills will be wasted.

Before we start discussing statistics in golf and how your stats can influence the way you practice and play the game, let's decide if you are more comfortable playing conservatively or aggressively. Take, for example, Tiger Woods and Phil Mickelson, arguably the two best players of the past twenty years. Tiger is similar to Jack Nicklaus when Jack was in his prime, just trying to get the ball in the fairway off the tee and then scoring with his great iron play and putting. Tiger probably has a better overall short game, especially bunker play, than Jack had. However, Tiger decided years ago that he's not the straightest driver in the world, so he developed his stinger, a little cut that goes low and is accurate. He *knows* he can get that shot into a tight fairway under pressure. It's like when a tennis player spins a second serve into play on a slow clay court, then tries to win the point from there.

Mickelson, on the other hand, is more like Arnold Palmer, who seemed to be going for broke on nearly every shot. Phil's strategy is to rip the driver as far as he can, even on narrow holes, and he's not afraid to hit the occasional errant tee shot because his attitude is that there are lots of birdies in the trees. He might even have a better chance of making birdie from the woods. At least, that's his mentality. Like Arnie, once Phil's in trouble, he thinks that's just an opportunity to show off. Ironically, Tiger has been marketed in the media as if he were Palmer, with the television networks repeatedly showing replays of dramatic slices from trouble with exaggerated, contorted follow-throughs, but in actuality Tiger plays a lot more like Nicklaus, hitting fairways and greens and playing strategically conservative golf. Making major championship venues easier off the tee in recent years—rewarding the bombers—is actually working against Tiger. It takes course management out of the equation or at least makes it less important. But that's not true on courses most amateurs play in competition. So, do you want to be a gambler, like Phil and Arnie, or would you rather be a patient, consistent ball-striker, like Tiger and Jack? Knowing your tendencies and your personality will help you to use your own stats to your advantage.

Back in the mid-nineties, I was working with Tom Kite, one of the most dedicated, disciplined students of the game to ever play the tour. Because of my background as a coach in lacrosse and basketball, I was very comfortable working with stats. For example, studying stats could tell us from where on the basketball court a player was a good shooter, so we'd give him a green light to shoot from there. We could determine more definitively a player's strengths and weaknesses, then tailor practice sessions to address those weaknesses. The PGA Tour, at the directive of a public relations firm, started a tour stats program in the early eighties, and my understanding was that the original reason for doing so was to get some publicity in newspapers because local papers weren't sending reporters to tournaments regularly. Other sports, such as football,

Be Conservative on Approach Shots

According to Scott Fawcett of Decade golf, who analyzed twenty thousand approach shots that Tiger Woods played on tour, Tiger hits his approaches at least 70 percent of the time to the fat side of the green, unless he has a scoring club in his hand. Tiger has followed Jack Nicklaus's example. Today, Justin Thomas, whom I have worked with, is likewise following in Tiger's footsteps, also playing conservative golf, hitting to the fat side of the green, unless he's hitting a scoring club. It's worked in the past with great champions, and it still works today, but it takes a great deal of discipline and patience to do so.

basketball, and baseball, all had a box score that you could send through the Associated Press wire service to any local newspaper. The PR firm didn't know a lot about golf, but decided to make up a box score. That's where the stats came from, and no one—not tour players or teachers or the media—knew what they meant. I had Kite send me the first ten or eleven years of tour stats, and I brought them to the Research Bureau at the University of Virginia, where I was director of the Sport Psychology Department. Dr. Bruce Gansneder, then a professor in the Curry School of Education and an expert in the Statistics and Research Bureau, did a regression analysis of the statistical information from the tour. Initially, we wanted to do two things: (1) predict scoring average, because for most players that was an important stat—if you had a good scoring average, you were going to have a good year, be highly ranked, and make a lot of money; and (2) study winning. We quickly realized that it is a lot easier to predict scoring average from stats than it is to predict winning. With winning, some luck is involved, where a player might hole a shot from off the green in a crucial situation, or hole a ninety-footer in the final few holes, or hit a tree and get a bounce in bounds and then make birdie instead of a double bogey. Maybe the other guys in contention got some bad breaks as well. The bottom line is, when you're analyzing stats, it's not as easy to predict winning as it is scoring average.

For the readers of this book, lowering your scoring average is clearly important to reaching your greatest potential. One of the first things you find out when you study the stats in golf is that, despite a common thought that we should learn to play the short game first, then the long game, a lot of evidence today suggests it's more important to learn how to hit the ball first—getting it in play off the tee consistently and hitting greens. In the old days, most players learned how to get the ball in the hole first, then maybe in their mid-to-late twenties or thirties they started learning how to hit the ball well. Some of it was that kids weren't allowed on the golf course as much as they are today, so young players spent a lot of time on the practice green chipping and putting. Today, with the advent of more accessible and better driving ranges, you see way more players learning how to hit the ball first, and later learning how to get the ball in the hole and developing a complete short game.

So the first thing you discover in studying the tour stats is you can predict about 67 percent of the variation in scoring average from the Greens Hit in Regulation (GIR) stat. Hitting greens in regulation is crucial in determining your scoring average. I tend to like the old way of looking at stats, versus the newer Strokes Gained approach. First of all, Strokes Gained is difficult for most players to understand, and second, it applies more to tour pros than amateurs because it uses the PGA Tour's ShotLink program. So we are going to focus on some basic tour stat categories that can apply to nontour golfers: Driving Distance (which is determined on just one or two holes per side), GIR, Scrambling Percentage, Putting, and Scoring Clubs.

Let's first examine GIR and how it might apply to prospective tour players and to your game if you don't have tour aspirations but want to achieve your greatest potential. The top 100 tour players are almost all hitting between 12.5 and 13.5 greens per round. So if you want to be playing on tour, you better be hitting 12½ to 13½ greens a round on 7,250-yard golf courses under tournament conditions. That's become a minimal requirement for playing on tour. Once you reach that benchmark, it's extremely difficult to do better than that. I've spent my career studying greatness and human potential, but I tell golfers the chances of your getting to 14 or 15 greens per round are slim to none, and it's probably a waste of your time and energy trying to achieve that. Once you can average 12½, it's a matter of maintenance. When Ben Hogan played, it was probably a huge advantage to being a great ball-striker because there weren't many of them then. But even at that time, players such as Hogan and Byron Nelson were averaging about 12½ greens per round. That stat hasn't changed much. The same is true with GIR and its relationship to Handicap Index. Not only has excellent ball-striking become a minimal requirement to play the tour, the same is true for getting your handicap down. If you were a scratch golfer hitting about four or five greens a round, you'd have to have the best short game in history.

It's not only about hitting greens, however—it's also about how bad your misses are. When you miss a green, are you just barely missing and are you missing in the best area to get it up and down? Or are you coming up well short, your ball plugging in the face of a bunker or maybe airmailing the green into an unplayable lie? When tour players miss a green, they miss pin-high a lot, and they are really good from there. Also, they sometimes technically miss a green but are on the fringe and putting, so the tour stat is a little inaccurate.

People often ask me what role driving the ball plays in hitting greens. I always answer that I want all my players to have a driver and one other club—whether it's a driving iron, a hybrid, a fairway wood—that they *know* they can hit the fairway with. Maybe they are thirty yards shorter with that club, but they are accurate with it and are confident they can hit it on the toughest driving holes they are ever going to have to play. So driving accuracy is important—probably more important in amateur golf than in pro golf, because at least in the last five years the courses on tour don't have rough that is that penal, the tree branches are cut up, not hanging down to the ground, the woods are usually cleaned up, and galleries and corporate tents save many wayward shots. Also, tour players are ridiculously good at hitting the ball tremendously high over trees and low under branches. In contrast, most amateur tournament golf, especially on the local level, has much tougher conditions off the fairway. If you want to become a good amateur or senior amateur player, you probably need to spend a lot of time developing a swing that will produce accuracy off the tee or find a club that will.

If you are going to use stats to design your practice and your course management, I want you to think about how you practice with your driver. Once you learn how to hit the driver, I would much rather you go on the golf course, say late in the day when it's not crowded, and find the toughest driving holes. On each tee, do your routine and hit three to five balls, go pick them up, and go to another tough driving hole. I don't think the driving range is a good place to practice hitting drives because there is no consequence for hitting a stray shot. When you're practicing, pretend you're in your next tournament, and when you're in a tournament, pretend you are in your favorite practice area, or your favorite practice holes on your home course. Think of it as your "happy place."

There are some great games to play on the course by yourself that have been productive for many of my players. While you are practicing on the course, play best ball with yourself. Hit three tee shots, and where your best ball finishes, play three balls from there. You hit the green, and you have three putts from the best shot, and you count your best putt. This is how you learn to shoot low. You find out what your potential is. Next, play worst ball with yourself. Again, hit three drives, but now you have to play your worst drive. Hit three shots from there, and again play your worst shot, on into the hole. This is good for learning how to score under pressure and getting mentally tough when you're not hitting the ball your best. It also teaches you to get disciplined with your routine. For example, if you hit two really good drives and then guide and steer your last drive into the trees, you've got to play that last one. If you make two putts, you've got to hole the third one. It's like what

What the Stats Don't Measure

The competitive spirit and how to fight—there is no stat that shows this, no stat for just finding a way to win, even if ugly, even if it's totally illogical to rational thinkers. There is no stat for making a putt to save par, or turning a double bogey into a great par. But they play an incredibly important role in someone becoming a successful player.

the basketball coaching legend Red Auerbach once said: "If you want to be a great basketball team, you have to figure out a way to win on the nights when you shoot thirty to thirty-five percent from the floor. The mediocre teams only win on the nights when they shoot fifty percent." That's what the short game is like in golf. If you want to be really good, you've got to be able to score when you're not hitting it your best.

For prospective tour pros, if you can drive it close to 300 yards or longer, driving accuracy on tour isn't as important because you are hitting wedges and short irons into the greens. But if you are a shorter hitter on tour and you're hitting it 270 max, then accuracy becomes extremely important, because hitting 4-, 5-, and 6-irons out of the rough will likely have a negative effect on your greens-hit stat. So driving is only significant in terms of how it impacts your GIR stat, which is the more important stat. Of course, if you're inconsistently wild off the tee and hitting it out of bounds or in water hazards, it's going to hurt your scoring average, so if that sounds like you, it's important to have an honest discussion with yourself and do something to become consistently more accurate off the tee.

That's where course management comes into play. Let's get back to Tiger and Phil as examples. What's crazy is that a lot of the online instruction videos, golf publications, and television shows want to use Tiger's and Phil's swings as examples. Well, Phil, for all his talent, is amazingly inaccurate off the tee, and to all those people who are chasing Tiger's swing, I say that Tiger probably uses the driver about two to four times per round.

His driving-accuracy stat might look pretty good at times, but he's often not hitting a driver. It would be a lot better stat if we knew how accurately players drive the ball when they hit driver. But the driving-accuracy stat is determined by how often you hit the fairway with your tee shot. Tiger hits a lot of irons off the tee, and he relies a lot on his bread-and-butter stinger to get the ball in play. So much of the time Tiger isn't even using the swing you are trying to copy when he has the driver in his hand. Then he tries to make birdie with the part of his game he's really good at. Throughout most of his career, Tiger scored low occasionally (such as his 61 in the 1999 Byron Nelson Championship), rarely shot over par, and scored 3 or 4 under to even par about 98 percent of the time. He won a lot of tournaments by wearing out the other players with his conservative consistency.

Phil has always taken a different approach. He misses a lot more cuts, has a lot more bad days, but shoots more super-low scores. (Phil shot a 59 at the PGA Grand Slam of Golf and is the only player on tour to have shot 60 or better at least three times.) If you're going to play like Phil, you better not let it bother you emotionally or mentally when you play poorly, you better not hate shooting high, and you better accept the off rounds with the great rounds, because to play like Phil and then be bothered when you make doubles and triples and high scores doesn't fit.

It's like Lanny Wadkins once told a reporter about worrying if he made cuts: "Cuts? I don't do corporate outings on weekends for two grand [the amount that corporate outings paid if you missed the cut]. If I can't win this weekend, I don't wanna play golf." That was Lanny's mentality. If you're going to play that way, really aggressively as he did, you can't be down in the dumps if you fail. You just have to have thick skin and not let it bother you. For Phil, his approach has its advantages, especially in certain conditions. It's no coincidence that of his six major victories, three are at Augusta National, which was more forgiving off the tee, and one was at the British Open when the conditions were hot and dry with manageable rough. Phil has never won the US Open, which at least until the last five years generally required a lot of accuracy off the tee. For most golfers (namely amateurs), I believe Tiger's and Jack's approach of putting the ball in the fairway off the tee is a much better model for course management. It will definitely lower the highest number you're going to shoot on a hole. The other advantage is that on tougher courses, where the fairways are tight and the rough is thick, this strategy will serve you well because it puts a premium on hitting fairways. As a result, you'll hit more greens, take fewer high numbers, and ultimately shoot lower scores.

So 67 percent of the variation in scoring average is affected by Greens Hit in Regulation, and the only thing we care about with the tee shot is how it is going to affect your Greens Hit stat. After GIR, the Driving Distance stat on tour doesn't tell you that much because it's measured only on a couple of holes. Some of the longest hitters on tour want to win that stat, so they always hit a driver on the measuring holes and try to bomb it. Other guys do not want to be known just for driving distance, so they go out of their way *not* to hit a driver on the Driving Distance holes.

The next category that will have a major impact on your game is Scrambling. Scrambling is defined as all shots from fifteen to twenty yards from the edge of the green. We'll just assume that most people who miss the green end up within fifteen to twenty steps from the putting surface. Let's break that down into four areas: chipping, pitching, lob shots, and bunker play. I have the players I work with rank in order from their best to their worst on those four wedge shots. It's common for my students to say, "Well, I'm a really good chipper, I'm pretty darn good with the lob shot, I'd rank bunker play third, and pitching fourth." And I'm thinking, *That's too bad, that's a real problem*.

I explain to these players that the order needs to be the opposite. They need to be a great pitcher of the ball and a solid bunker player. But the lob shot is not as important, and chipping today is almost irrelevant. Because of the way courses are maintained today, green committees and superintendents have virtually taken chipping out of the game. They are cutting the fringes and areas around the green super tight. I don't know if the superintendents or the USGA intended to make chipping obsolete, but it's becoming that way. I tell my students I wouldn't waste my time practicing chipping anymore. If you are three to seven feet off the green, you can putt it today at most well-conditioned golf courses. Or maybe use your hybrid with a putting stroke. Until Mickelson came along and made the lob shot a big deal, you couldn't think of a great champion who hit lob shots, so you don't have to be a great lob wedge player to win tournaments. In short-game practice, I suggest you spend most of your time on pitching and bunker play. I would rank pitching ahead of bunker play because you tend to have more pitches in a given round than bunker shots. Of course, you have to look at your own stats and weaknesses. If you are a lousy bunker player and sometimes leave it in the bunker or skull it out, get yourself a good bunker lesson and then allot your practice time accordingly. But in general, and for most players, I would make pitching my most important short-game shot.

You need to have a medium-trajectory pitch shot, lofting it a bit with backspin, for those occasional times you miss on the short side, and you need a pitch shot that releases and runs for the times you are pitching a long way, say to a back pin or perhaps on a tier. As you are learning, I would like you to start practicing off good lies, then thin lies, then off dirt cart paths, or sanded divots or just dirt, but you should find the worst lies possible so that any lie in a tournament looks easy. I want you to get really good at those two pitch shots so you can go to any golf course and have a clear, quiet mind. You can look at it statistically. If you are missing twelve or fourteen greens a round and getting most of those shots up and down, you can see that it's easy to save twelve or fourteen shots in a round. It's also demoralizing to your opponents in match play. But if you're missing that many greens and never saving par, your score can add up fast, especially if you're chunking or skulling your pitches. You can also hit thirteen greens and not get it up and down four out of five chances and shoot a quick 76, rather than 71 or 72.

Again, I don't want the players I work with keeping stats every day and going crazy with the numbers. But I think it's a good idea to look at your stats every once in a while to understand your game and guide your practice sessions. How you organize your pitching practice time is important. It needs to be efficient, but it also should encourage your sense of feel and promote confidence for when you execute the same shots on the course. It's okay in the beginning to hit a pile of balls to the same pin or cup. As you get better, you need to hit to a different cup every time so you're bringing imagination into the process and not just trying to repeat the same impact, the same trajectory, the same roll. Now with each ball you've got to hit a different trajectory, a different spin, to a different target, which brings your creativity into your short game. Then, ultimately, you've got to start practicing with one ball with your wedges and your putter, and you've got to get great at getting your ball up and down. It's not about being able to hit a pitch shot, it's the mindset that you can get it up and down from everywhere. So many people think, *I'm practicing my pitching*, but they need to practice the mindset of getting the ball up and down. That is what *real* golf is about.

You're probably better off going out on the golf course (maybe late in the day when it's not crowded) and practicing real pitch-shot situations from various lies and distances from the pin. This is a great opportunity to practice staying in the moment and making your next shot your best shot. I want you to practice

Playing Great Is Scoring Great

I find myself saying the following to players all the time: "Playing great is scoring great. You cannot play great if you don't score." But I hear something different a lot: "Well, I really played great today, I just didn't score." And I say, "That's impossible." What they mean is they *hit the ball well and didn't score*. Just because they drove it beautifully and hit a lot of greens doesn't always mean they played great. Playing great means you find a way to get the ball in the hole. That's what truly playing golf is, and the best players adopt that mindset.

uphill lies, downhill lies, sidehill lies, from various lengths of grass, and so on. For transfer of training, practicing getting it up and down is going to give you the best results. You will hit fewer balls, so your quantity will go down, but your quality will go up. Of course, if you are practicing on the golf course, you need permission from the golf staff, you must stay safely clear of other golfers, and you need to fix divots and ball marks. However, great players, from Bobby Jones to Justin Thomas, have been doing this for a long time. A lot of modern courses have designed amazing short-game areas that are good for enticing and selling memberships, but I've noticed that once people join, they don't tend to spend much time there. The bottom line is, if you want to separate yourself from the other players and reach your fullest potential, you need to put the time into the short game.

Regarding sand shots, players can spend six hours in the practice bunker and still not get every type of shot and lie they might face during a round of golf. So most good players spend a lot of time practicing different bunker shots on the golf course, from every lie—uphill, downhill, sidehill—from different kinds of sand, different amounts and texture of sand, until they get good at it. It's like the story that Gary Player's sons tell about their dad, who missed many a dinner on his ranch in South Africa because he refused to come into the house in the evening until he holed three bunker shots (he had a short course on his property with great bunkers and greens). There has never been a better bunker player in the history of the game. You need to spend about 70 percent of your practice time on your short game and your wedges. If you don't do this, you probably won't reach your dreams as a golfer. If you have limited time, devote it to pitching and bunker play, and develop the mindset that you can get it up and down from everywhere. I want you to get to a point where missing a green has no meaning to you, you have no fear of missing a green, and no fear of being in a bunker. You are almost glad when your ball is in a bunker because it's an opportunity to show off your short game.

Then, in addition to pitching and bunker play, spend about twenty minutes a day on your putting. Again, the stats tell the story. The easiest way to improve your putting is to hit your pitch shots close. It doesn't take a genius to realize that if you're pitching the ball to three feet as opposed to seven, you will make a lot more putts no matter how good a putter you are. If you are hitting it to three feet versus twelve feet, it's mind-boggling how big a difference that is in scoring. But having said that, if all the tour players are hitting between 12.5 and 13.5 greens per round, the players who are scoring the lowest and winning tournaments are the ones hitting it the closest and making the most putts.

So that takes you from 67 percent of the variation in scoring to 88 percent. If your goal was to lower the highest score you could shoot, you would hit more greens and you would have a really good up-and-down game. For example, if you're hitting ten greens a round and you're getting it up and down six out of eight times, you are no doubt going to lower the highest number you can shoot. If you're hitting ten greens and getting up and down only two out of eight times, you're looking at shooting 78 rather than 74. Yet, so many golfers practice only the long game and forget about the short game. Make sure you are not one of those golfers!

Now, once you get to there, the other 12 percent from our stats is about how many birdies you are making with your scoring clubs. (This is for tour players and low-handicap amateurs; for higher handicappers, it might be how many pars you are making with your scoring clubs.) What is a scoring club? Years ago, at a Golf Digest Instruction Panel meeting, I asked Sam Snead, Cary Middlecoff, and Paul Runyan what they considered to be a scoring club on tour. They said it's an 8-iron through sand wedge (they didn't use lob wedges then). I asked them why they called them scoring clubs, and they responded that you can't score great if you're not great with those clubs. Today, players are hitting it so long on tour that they consider the scoring clubs to be their pitching wedge through their lob wedge, and most carry three or four wedges, often with lofts of 48, 52, 56, and 60 degrees. Mickelson carries a 64. I would recommend working with a respected club-fitter to be sure the lofts on your wedges are evenly spaced apart. For most amateurs, the scoring clubs are probably still a three-quarter 8-iron through the lob wedge.

To start scoring as low as possible, you've got to start hitting those scoring clubs closer to the pin. I want you to be conservative off the tee, getting the ball into the fairway. Then with your approaches to the green with a 7-iron down to your hybrids and fairway woods, pick a conservative target—the middle of the green or toward the middle of the green—and get your Greens Hit stat up. When I talk about a conservative target, I don't mean playing scared or swinging scared. If you are swinging scared, that's a real problem. *I want you to make an aggressive, confident swing to a conservative target.* That's playing smart, strategic golf. I call it "conservative strategy, cocky swing." However, when you have an approach shot with a scoring club, I want you to be *very aggressive*, in an attack mode, taking dead aim, to quote the great teacher Harvey Penick. That's when you're firing at flags. It's *party time.* If you want to get really good, you have to make more birdies with your scoring clubs. This mentality will take some pressure off your game, and this is where you start lowering the lowest number you can shoot.

Tour players and low-handicap amateurs might have about ten scoring club approaches in a given round. They need to take advantage of that. For some weaker players who don't hit it that far, it's a little different. They have to be a lot better with their fairway woods, or their hybrids or their medium irons, in addition to their wedges. I worked with Vicki Goetze on the LPGA Tour years ago, and she could hit her 7-wood closer to the pin than some men could hit their wedges. She was small in stature, had a relatively low swing speed, but she was deadly with her high-lofted fairway woods. She won two US Women's Amateur Championships, defeating Annika Sorenstam for her second title.

If your goal is to become an exceptional golfer, you need to practice these scoring shots every day. If you are a little off with these clubs, you might hit it to twenty-five feet instead of five. I can show you stats of all kinds of players who have nice golf swings and are good ball-strikers, but they don't hit their wedges any closer than they hit their 5- or 6-iron. If you are *missing* greens with your wedges, it might be costing you *two* shots per miss. If you're hitting it to twenty feet instead of eight, it's probably costing you a shot to a shot and a half. It makes a difference if you're hitting them close. If you're totally dialed in, you might get a couple that are tap-ins in eighteen holes. If you have a swing that is good enough to hit a driver, you can learn to hit a wedge close.

Dave Pelz, the short-game teaching pro who was also a NASA scientist and has worked a lot with Mickelson, once noted that for a golfer who shoots 96 on average, the break-down of shots goes something like this: forty putts, twenty wood shots (drivers and fairway woods), fourteen iron shots, nineteen wedges, and three "others." So why does that same golfer spend so much time banging the driver on the range and not practicing the wedge game? It's so important to put in your practice time on these shots. I'd like you to spend at least an hour a day on this part of your game, and if you want to get better quicker, spend more time on it. I tell the players I work

Rotella's Six Rules for Analyzing Stats

1. Work your tail off to hit twelve to thirteen greens per round, not to achieve driving distance.
2. Short game—develop a medium- and a low-trajectory pitch shot.
3. Learn to be a great bunker player.
4. Practice putting twenty minutes a day.
5. Focus on your scoring clubs (at least an hour a day), any club with a *W* on it.
6. Like free-throw shooting in basketball, it's boring to practice the scoring clubs, but if you want to be great, you must have them dialed in.

with that a typical short-game practice session would be two to two and a half hours, with at least an hour with your scoring clubs and twenty minutes with your putter. The rest would be bunker play and pitches around the green, working on the two types of pitch shots we discussed earlier.

You will make more progress faster if you have immediate and accurate feedback when practicing your scoring clubs. I also want you to develop a full-swing shot and a three-quarter shot with each of these clubs. That is how you can produce shots that go the correct distance more consistently. You need to have a way of measuring how far your ball went on each practice shot. Your eyes can usually tell how far right or left your shot went, but distance is harder to determine. Some players rely on a TrackMan, even for shots of less than 100 yards. Some use one of the less expensive analyzers that you can connect to your phone. Some use their GPS range finder. Some put towels down at various yardages and measure with their eyes. And some use a caddie or a friend to go downrange when it's not crowded or on an empty golf hole and relay back the exact distances of each shot through each other's cell phones. Most tour players are trying to get their three-quarter shots to go at about a thirty-degree trajectory. That's quite a bit lower than a full swing, which lets them control their distance better. The goal is to increase predictability with your pitch shots and also with your full and three-quarter shots with your scoring clubs.

It is important to have consistent impact on each shot so you can have a predictable trajectory, so you can know how far the shot goes, so there's no fear when the pin is tucked behind a bunker or on a back tier. Every day you've been measuring, and you know exactly how far the ball goes with each club, and you have a full swing and a three-quarter swing to achieve that. I don't encourage you to go haywire with half swings or one-third swings. At least until you are a scratch golfer, just go with a full shot and three-quarter shot. You have to take a hard look at *your* game.

My dad, who lived a very long life and played golf to age one hundred, would almost always have a thirty- to seventy-yard third shot into every par 4. He'd have the same distance for his fourth shot on the par 5s. If he was good with that club throughout the round, it could mean a 16-shot difference for his score that day. It was amazing how not being able to reach the green didn't affect his score that much. He could make a par or a bogey and go to the next hole. A lot of golfers are similar to that, where that length pitch shot could be the most important part of their game for scoring as low as possible. Therefore, regarding *your* game, for the next two weeks keep your own stats. After each round, go back through each shot on every hole. Determine which clubs you hit the most on average. Then ask yourself, "On which shots am I giving away the most strokes? Which clubs are helping me the most, and which ones are hurting me?"

I ask good amateurs and even tour pros to do the same thing. I'm amazed with good players how seldom they are hitting the ball out of bounds, yet they only want to work on their driver. I tell them, you're already as good as you need to be off the tee, and even if you're not confident with your driver one day, you have an option off the tee. You can always hit another, more forgiving club to get the ball into the fairway. But if you have a short pitch over a bunker to a tight pin, you can't putt it through the bunker. So you better be good at that shot.

Another thing I want you to do regarding your own game is to take your worst five rounds and record their stats, then take your best five rounds and do the same. Compare them and ask yourself what the difference is between your best rounds and your worst. I would venture to say that most people find that they're making birdies with their scoring clubs and they're getting it up and down better in their best rounds. But don't just take my word for it. Have a good look at your own stats. For instance, when I examine the stats of some of the amateurs I work with, it's amazing what I am able to tell them. I'll have them write down every club they hit on every shot for one entire round. First I go through their tee shots. It's amazing how often they will have no penalty shots off the tee and no drives that cost them. I have them write down how many chances they had to approach the green with an 8-iron through lob wedge. It's almost always somewhere between ten and twelve chances. I have them record that. Then we add up how many times they got it up and down when they missed a green. When you start adding it up and analyzing it, you can quickly see that if they were sharper with their scoring clubs, they'd have a lot more opportunities to make birdie. If they got it up and down more often, they'd save a lot of strokes and really change their score.

The great Mexican player and Hall of Famer Lorena Ochoa dominated the LPGA Tour before she retired at age twenty-eight to have a family. She wasn't afraid to shoot low, and her birdies often came in spurts. She used her stats to determine how she practiced. In an article in 2020, she told *Golf Digest*:

> The better you know yourself, the sooner you're going to start dominating. You should always work on your weaknesses. Some people know what their weaknesses are but don't touch them. They get lazy. I always ask myself, "What is the weakness?" If I was having trouble with sixty-five yards, or a 4-iron, or driver with a fade, then I'd spend two to three hours at the range so that I dominate those weaknesses. Then I have the ability. I know I'll be able to hit them in competition. Once you get traveling, you start doing the easy things, you forget about the difficult things that you don't like to do. What is key is to take care of your weaknesses really quickly. That way you have more space to improve, and that's not just true in golf, it's also true in life.

Use what you learn from studying your stats to guide your practice and your on-course strategy. It will make your practice time and play time more beneficial and rewarding, so you can begin to achieve your greatest potential with your game and reach for your highest dreams.

CHAPTER 10

On Becoming a Great Putter

Science is in the mind; feeling is in the hands. You must see it go in.

—Jack Nicklaus

Great putting is much more about attitude than technique. You really have to feel that you're having a lot of fun on the greens. I want you to be instinctive and unconscious when you're putting, reacting rather than thinking analytically. To help the players I work with understand what I'm talking about, I often start by playing a little game of catch with them—with a set of keys. With each toss I step back a step or two. They take a quick look at wherever I put my hand and hit it with the keys. Every time, they hit my hand with just the right amount of speed so as not to hurt me. I usually say, "Isn't that amazing? What a great athlete you are! You just casually looked at my hand, you never thought about aiming at my hand, you never gave any conscious thought about how hard to throw it. You just did it. So we don't have to wonder if you have a great touch. We already know that. We just have to get you to the point with your putting where you feel the same way as when you threw those keys to me." It's about developing an attitude for putting that allows you to be unconscious and react instinctively to what you are seeing on the greens.

In the previous chapters, we talked a lot about what you can learn from coaches in other sports and how they're able to bring out exceptional performances in their players. I believe the way great athletes carry themselves and approach what they do is analogous to golf. I've often said that many golfers act like serious uptight nerds when they would be a lot better off acting like stud muffins or studettes. You need to stop thinking so

How Denny McCarthy Goes Unconscious

I work with the young tour player Denny McCarthy, who exemplifies the approach of feeling unconscious on the greens. Denny led the tour in strokes gained in 2019 and 2020. He has told me that he just sees a spot and a line to the hole. He unconsciously reacts to what his eyes look at without any concern about the outcome. It has helped him become a great putter. Without hesitation, he sets up and makes his stroke, which helps him putt with extreme confidence.

analytically and unathletically and start playing golf using an athletic mindset and having confidence in your ability. This applies not only to your ball-striking, but also to your putting. You might not think putting is athletic, but this is where you should be the most instinctive and unconscious. I want you to treat putting as if it *is* athletic. Let me explain.

I've been around some really good putters over the years, and I've learned that the ones who rise above the rest simply react to the putt they see, rather than overthink it. Most don't take a lot of time analyzing things, and they certainly don't spend much time between their last look at the target and stroking the putt. Just as great athletes in other sports—say football or basketball—sense an upcoming play and let their body react, great putters do the same thing. When a grounder is hit to a shortstop in baseball, he doesn't think through how his feet are moving to get to the ball, or if he's going to backhand it, or once the ball is in his glove how he's going to grab it with his throwing hand. As he starts to throw, he doesn't spend any time at all thinking about how he's holding the ball in his fingers, or how his wrist is positioned as he cocks his arm, or how fast he needs to move his arm as he fires to first base. It's all instinctive and natural. If he did start to analyze any part of the motion, he'd probably throw the ball in the dirt or over the first baseman's head.

Putting should be no different. Putt either with your eyes (which means you are looking at the target and reacting), or with your mind's eye (seeing the target in your mind and reacting to that image). As great putters are over the ball, they are reacting instinctively to what their eyes have looked at. Are you seeing the ball tracking along your intended line and going in the cup? It's amazing how various great putters see putts differently before they make their stroke (see the sidebar "What's in Your Head?" on page 174). Some see a thin line from the ball to the hole; some see a wide line; some see a spot and try to roll the ball over that spot; some focus on where the ball will enter the cup. It doesn't matter, as long as it makes sense to your brain.

Jack Nicklaus, one of the greatest clutch putters of all time, wanted an image in his mind. Once Jack's image was clear, and only when it was clear, did he take the putter back. You couldn't put Jack's routine on a stopwatch because he waited until he had the picture. A lot of people will say to me that Jack didn't have a routine, and I have to explain that, yes, he did, but it's a subtle difference. His routine was that he was reacting to a picture. Tiger Woods, who has made an incredible number of big putts dating back to his junior golf and amateur days, is similar. He has said he "putts to the picture," which his father taught him as a young boy. I don't care which way you do it, but a lot of people tell me that they can see a picture sometimes, but not all the time. I tell them that's no good. If you do not see a picture in your mind's eye *every time*, then that should not be your process. You need a more specific, consistent routine.

Davis Love III, who has made his share of great putts during his career, including a six-footer on the eighteenth green to clinch the Ryder Cup in 1993 at The Belfry and a twelve-footer to cap off a brilliant PGA Championship victory in 1997 under a rainbow at Winged Foot, doesn't hesitate on his routine. As soon as he's taken his last look at his line, the putter starts going back. We worked hard at creating this routine. I don't want any hesitation over the ball. I don't want any conscious thought between your last look at the target and taking the putter back. Most people want to start thinking consciously right then, maybe to make sure to take the putter back correctly, or to second-guess their read, or to hit it hard enough, or to keep their left wrist flat. That's the worst possible moment because you're interfering with your athleticism and your reaction to the target. That's when the mind can get overactive and sabotage a good, confident stroke. I want you to get all your thinking done before you get over the ball. Davis told me it's like those silver weighted balls lined up on strings you see in the convenience shops in the Atlanta airport. One ball hits another, causing a chain reaction. He also noted that his trapshooting instructor at Sea Island, Georgia, where Davis grew up and still lives, always wanted the shotgun moving along with the target as Davis pulled the trigger. No hesitation. This is what I mean by being athletic.

So much of today's instruction about putting is how to make a perfect stroke. I'm much more concerned with your attitude about putting. I often begin my putting seminars by telling people, "Stand up and put your right hand up in front of you. Now take your hand and arm and move it back and forth." Without fail, everyone does it. "That's a perfect putting stroke," I tell them. "Why would you spend hours working on learning how to do that if you already know how to do it? It's no different just because we put a putter in your hand." My next point is usually that a putting stroke happens in response to a picture in your mind or in response to what your eyes actually see. Do not try to make a correct or perfect stroke. You have to let it happen.

I'm very big on having consistent routines, so how do you develop one in putting? Again, we can learn from great athletes in other sports where they must initiate the movement: serving in tennis, pitching in baseball, placekicking in football, and free-throw shooting in basketball. The best performers have a consistent routine with no hesitation. Take Kyle Guy, the Sacramento Kings point guard who played for the University of Virginia. In the 2019 NCAA Championship semifinal game against Auburn, Virginia was down by 2 points in the final seconds. With just 0.6 seconds left on the clock, Guy got fouled and was awarded three free throws. Miraculously, he made them all to win the game. For each shot, his routine never changed, and he also never hesitated. One bounce, look, and shoot. You can do the same in your putting routine. It doesn't matter what kind of routine you have. I just want it to be exactly the same every time, as long as, whatever it is, you take very little time from your last look at the target until you come back to the ball and take the putter back. It's not just the same routine, but also having the same rhythm and flow to it, no matter the distance of the putt, whether it's a thirty-footer or a three-footer. Write down the process you have developed, including aligning your putterface, positioning your feet, your body, getting your

Learn How to Make a Par, and Accept a Bogey

For a low-handicap player or a tour pro, some patience is needed in learning how to make a par and how to accept a bogey. Everyone who gets good at golf has learned how to make a par or at least save a bogey. They don't turn two bad shots into a double bogey or a triple. Some of it is you learn to get the ball up and down. Some of it is you make a putt to save a score. Some of it is you learn that "sometimes I have to accept a bogey, and it's okay." I've got some buddies who hit the ball nicely, but they've never learned how to make a par or take a bogey and stay in the round.

eyes over the ball, and so forth. If you take practice strokes, make sure it's the same number every time. In addition to writing down your routine, on the putting green you might even say it out loud to yourself. It's helpful to tell it to somebody else. That will encourage you to stick to your routine and to approach all your putts the same way. For example, after Matt Wolff made a solid eight-footer to shoot 65 in the third round of the 2020 US Open, which tied the lowest score ever in a US Open at Winged Foot, he was asked if he approached that putt differently. "Nope," he said. "To me, it's just another putt. I've trained myself to treat every putt the same."

Once you have your setup and your routine is consistent, becoming a great putter is mostly about attitude. Brad Faxon, known as one of the best putters of all time, started working with me in his first year on tour, back in 1983. He described what I taught him for writer Bob Cullen in *Travel + Leisure Golf* magazine in 2002: "I really believe putting is an attitude thing. By this, I mean that how a golfer thinks is more important than anything else." Brad pointed out that when he walks toward the green and starts reading the putt, he weighs a lot of factors almost subconsciously—the slope, the speed of the green, the wind. He said he doesn't permit himself to overread the putt. He wants to be decisive. His putting falters when he starts to second-guess his initial read.

"To me, putting is very visual," Brad continued. "I take a last look at the target line and let my stroke go. I don't worry about speed. I let my instincts and skills take care of that." Brad is striving for a delicately balanced frame of mind in which he's focused, but not focused too tightly. Meticulous about his routine, but not overly careful, he wants the putt to go in. He believes it will go in. But he doesn't want to be upset if it misses. "I want to not try very hard," he said. "That's when I putt great."

When Brad is putting well, he almost always has to mark the ball when he misses his first putt because he's run it too far past the hole for a tap-in. Also, when he putts his best, he usually has at least one three-putt for the round. He accepts that, knowing that when he's in the right frame of mind, the birdie putts made will greatly outnumber the three-putts.

It's like I've often said, if you're afraid of three-putting, you'll two-putt your life away. Brad and I have worked together for a long time. He says that a lot of kids develop fear because a parent or an older friend tells them they have to stop running their putts so far past the hole. He realized kids have no fear when they putt, and you've got to keep that attitude your whole life. Everyone who was a pretty good player had his mind where it needed to be when he was twelve. Most people get way too conscious, too fearful, as they get older. I've tried to keep Brad from ever growing up when it comes to putting.

Adults can learn from kids in other ways regarding putting. I have to remind adults to have more putting contests, like kids do. As we get older, we tend to work with devices and drills, and we get away from playing games and having contests on the practice green. Likewise, I want to see golfers, as they get closer to tournament time or on the day of the tournament, get rid of their devices and spend a lot more time doing their routine on the putting green and practicing *making* putts.

It's the same with reading greens. Kids are almost always great green readers, and no one has told them how. It's instinctive and they have no fear of misreading. Tour pros tell me that in pro-ams they always read the greens much better for their amateur partners because they don't feel pressure if they make a mistake. It's only the Wednesday pro-am. Try caddying for a good friend for eighteen holes. You're just having fun. There's no fear. I bet you'll experience the same thing and will read the putts really well.

Some golfers have told me they almost don't want to hit a good approach shot within a few feet of the hole because they're afraid they'll miss the putt. As they walk up to the green, they start worrying about what others in their group will think. Remember, no one else cares. Five seconds after you putt, people have forgotten about you. Or some players might fear if they miss a short putt on the first hole, it will set a bad tone with their putting for the day and they'll lose their confidence. That philosophy won't work in competition unless you always make every makeable putt early in the round, so you need to change that attitude toward putting. Great putters, as soon as they hit the ball on the green, start thinking about how much fun it's going to be to make the putt. I teach the players I coach to tell themselves, "Now it's party time. This is where the real fun begins." It's like when you're getting ready to go to a party, you're in the shower, then you're getting dressed, and you're already anticipating how much fun it's going to be. I want you to feel this way when you walk onto the green. This is the game within the game. I want you to say to yourself, *This is when I can separate myself from the other players.*

Again, putting is mostly about attitude. You need to love one-putting more than you hate three-putting. I want you to love making birdies. Love putting for all eighteen holes. Love bending over and picking the ball out of the cup. I want you to putt without worrying about having to make the comebacker. If you are thinking about missing the comebacker, you are not staying in the present moment. You are already anticipating the next putt and its impact on your score and are not focused on the process. I don't mind if you leave a putt half a ball short. That happens sometimes. It's not okay, however, if you left it short because you were concerned about running it by.

I want you to have an attitude of indifference about the outcome. After the putt, it's about accepting what happened. Even if the ball didn't go in, if you executed your process the way you intended, it's a "Rotella Make." Maybe the ball hit an imperfection on the green, or the wind kept the ball out, or you simply misread the putt. Pat yourself on the back for sticking with your routine, visualizing the putt and focusing on reacting to the target unconsciously. You cannot let results dictate how you feel about your putting. If you're not making putts, stick to your routine and get looser and more assured of yourself as you go along. The tendency is to do the opposite and tighten up if they're not falling. By looser and more assured, I do not mean making your stroke loose—I mean making your attitude more relaxed, almost as if you are trying less and caring less as the round goes on. Have a soft look and a quiet mind—don't stare at the target. Putt like it doesn't matter. Trust your instincts, even on the read. Great putters, as soon as they're walking onto the green, already know what the putt does. Believe in your first instinct, which is based on confidence and trust, or you will tend to invent break that doesn't exist.

The right attitude also means loving the greens you are putting on. You can't let the condition of the greens control your mind. If everyone you are playing with, whether it's in a tournament or just your weekend group, is complaining about the speed or the quality of the greens, you will have a clear advantage if you do not fall into the same trap. Early in my

What's in Your Head?

What do you see as you're over the putt? Many of the game's top putters have described their visuals. You can—and should—make up your own.

Pat Bradley: She thought she had a laser beam from between her eyes. She felt as if she were burning a laser in the green from the ball to the target, and the ball couldn't get out of the burn.

Nick Price: He looked at the target and then at the ball. In his mind, he pretended to have a camera in his left ear. So when he was looking at the ball, he was seeing an image of the target.

Bobby Locke: He picked a spot and saw every putt as straight and let the green break the ball into the hole. Unless the putt was indeed straight, his look was always at his spot rather than the actual cup.

Raymond Floyd: He saw the ball rolling up the slope and curling into the hole: "I always see it falling into the hole. I strongly believe you can will a putt into the hole, just as you can by negative thinking will it out of the hole."

Brad Faxon: He sees an action track, a thin line going from the ball to the hole. When he takes his stance, he sees the ball starting on that line.

My daughter, Casey (who played college golf for Notre Dame): She is a big Beatles fan and imagined putting to Ringo's lips.

career, when I taught in the Golf Digest Schools, I spent quite a bit of time with the legendary teacher Davis Love Jr., who was a very good player in his own right. Davis recounted rooming with Gary Player to save money in their early days on tour. They were playing a tournament somewhere in the South on super-slow Bermuda greens. Davis thought they were some of the worst greens he'd ever seen. But every evening Player would come back to the room and say, "Man, I love these slow greens. They are made for me." The following week, they drove north to the next tournament, which was played on unbelievably slick bent-grass greens. Again, every evening Player would come back to the room and say how much he enjoyed the greens: "I just love putting on these fast greens. All I have to do is get the ball rolling and it goes in." At the time Davis thought, *Well, you can't have it both ways.* But this is the way great athletes think. It comes down to your free will and creating your own reality. Convince yourself you are a good putter on slow, medium, or fast greens, and you will have a distinct edge over most other golfers.

So how do you acquire an attitude of not trying so hard when the goal is to make as many putts as possible? It's counterintuitive. I don't want to you think, *I gotta make it.* Don't build up the importance of certain putts. If anything, downplay them. Even in match play. If a putt is to win a hole or to tie a hole, just tell yourself it doesn't matter and go through your routine. Just visualize the ball going in the cup. You're not trying hard to make it while you're over the ball, you're just keeping things moving. It's like the run-and-shoot in basketball. You're looking and reacting. Only have eyes for where you want the ball to go. Try this Look & Shoot game on the practice green: Put down nine balls about twelve feet from a hole. Putting one ball at a time, take one look and go. Get looser, freer, and more assured with each ball. By the sixth ball, you'll probably be freed up, and you'll be amazed how well you are rolling it. Both your distance and direction will be great. Now you are reacting to the target.

You don't have to be born a great putter; you can make yourself one. Here are some other games you can play on the practice green to make yourself a better putter: Practice tons of short putts, so you see the ball going in the hole a lot. Instead of spending hours practicing straight, six-foot putts, which tends to deaden the imagination, have fun making big, breaking putts at different speeds to see that there is not one line to make a putt on. People who are into technique want to practice straight putts because it reinforces whether their stroke is perfect. But it kills their imagination and their touch. You'll develop your instinct for judging speed and playing the right amount of break for various speeds if you spend more time on the big right-to-left and left-to-right putts. It brings your imagination to life, which you need to become a great putter. It shows there is not one line.

The week of the Masters in 2008, I worked with Trevor Immelman of South Africa. I had arranged for us to get together with Ben Crenshaw up in the Champions locker room to discuss putting. Ben talked about how he loved putting at Augusta because he could make a putt using five to seven different lines, depending on the speed the ball was hit. I believe a light went on in Trevor's head, and he proceeded to win that week. Faxon does a similar drill. For years I've spent time with Brad playing this game: he will make the same putt at three different speeds. I have always encouraged him to practice hitting putts with his driver or his sand wedge, which lowers his expectations and helps him realize he can make putts with anything if his head is right. Sometimes we'd use a 2-iron, turn it around sideways, and hit putts on the narrow end of the head. You'll be amazed how well you roll the ball with a club other than your putter. Try the Paul Runyan approach. Paul, one of the most respected short-game gurus, who defeated Sam Snead 8 & 7 in the 1938 PGA Championship final when it was still at match play, envisioned short putts hitting the back of the cup; medium putts the low-back part of the cup liner; and long putts falling in the front edge.

Straight Back and through or on an Arc?

If you feel it's necessary to work on your stroke, at least do it without a ball and maybe go stand in front of a mirror. That is how and when to work out any mechanical issues. You can get into a huge argument on what a correct stroke is: Do you take it straight back and through? Or do you make a little arc or a big arc? Some people, as Bobby Locke used to do, take it back a little inside and then down the line through impact. Whatever stroke you want, just get a putter that causes that to happen without you trying to make it happen. If you want a bigger arc, get a flatter putter. If you want it to go straight back and straight through, get a more upright putter. If you want a little arc, you can probably buy a standard putter off the shelf. But don't buy a putter that does one thing and try to make it do something else. The right putter will do it for you if you stay out of your own way and let it happen.

Early in the week of the 2011 Open Championship at Royal St George's, Darren Clarke found me on the practice green. He told me that he was in such a dire place with his putting that he felt he had to hit his approaches to within a foot of the cup to make any birdies. He wasn't making any putts to speak of. His speed control was terrible and he wasn't making solid contact. He was close to desperate. "Doc, they're missing as soon as they leave the putterface," he lamented. "I'm really struggling." My goal for the tournament was to get Darren to putt like he did when he was a teenager. I wanted him to feel unconscious when he putted. In fact, we took this approach with his putting to his whole game. With his entire game I wanted him to have fun and look and react to the target with his eyes with no concern for the outcome. When you're having fun, you tend to be more unconscious and process oriented. When you get serious, you tend to get conscious and outcome oriented.

"You know how to putt, so stop pretending you don't," I said. "And you have to stop trying to do what someone else tells you is correct. You've got to putt like Darren Clarke putts." I reminded him that the times he putted well he got out of his own way and putted by instinct. "See it and hit it, and accept whatever it does," I said. "At the moment you're fighting a war with this thing . . . and you're not winning." Darren acknowledged that he was not allowing himself to be unconscious as he putted. He was thinking, changing his mind, doing everything except what used to come naturally.

I took Darren back to some basic things we had worked on in the past. I grabbed a golf ball and started playing catch with him. I'd put my hand up and he'd hit it every time with the ball. "When you threw the ball, did you think about where your weight was?" I asked. "Did you aim your throwing hand?" He shook his head no. "Not only did you hit my hand every time, you threw the ball at just the right pace so it didn't hurt when I caught it," I continued. "The point is, you unconsciously knew how to throw it to me without thinking about aim or how hard to throw it so that you wouldn't hurt me, and that's what your putts will do if you stop thinking about them consciously. If you worry about leaving it short, you will gun it, and if you worry about running it by the hole, you'll ease up on it. Just believe that if you looked and trusted, then it would go at the right speed and on the right line; you don't have to tell yourself *how* to do it."

Then I had Darren hit some putts. I asked him to have fun putting unconsciously, to do his preparation behind the ball, picking a target and seeing his line distinctly, and not getting up to the ball until he was clear and committed. "Then just look where you want it to go and hit it—don't change your mind when you're over the ball," I said. "If you even think about changing your mind once you are over the ball, you have to walk away and start the process all over again. For example, if you start to question the line, worry about the speed, et cetera, you have to get away from it and start all over again. Sometimes on TV, if one of the players I work with walks away from a putt, the commentators say, 'Oh, he's got bad thoughts in his

Downplay Putts, rather than Build Them Up

Building Up Putts

- I have to make this putt to win the hole. It's really big.
- I get a stroke here, so I need to make this one.
- This one's crucial, my partner is in his pocket.
- I can't afford to let this opportunity get away.
- It's the first hole, I need to get off to a great start.
- It's the final hole, this one's really huge.

Versus . . .

Downplaying Putts

- Man, this is just another putt.
- This one is just like on the practice green when I was warming up.
- I'm going to have a million putts just like this.
- Just have fun on this one.
- Wow, putting is a lot of fun.
- I don't care if I make it or miss it, just do my process.

head' or 'This isn't good.' But I am applauding. I'm thinking, *I know they just saved this putt, they are disciplined today.* I don't want you thinking about a routine. I want you to look at the target and let it happen. If you do that, a great routine will be yours. I want you to be unconsciously reacting to what you've just looked at, and I don't want you taking time when you come back to the ball, because that is when most people are tempted to turn on their conscious mind and start thinking. Keep your conscious brain switched off. Your speed and line will take care of themselves."

Soon Darren was hitting the ball squarely in the center of the putterface, his speed was good, and he was making his share. I had him putt from five feet with the heel of the putter, then the toe, and he made several in a row. Then I asked him to putt a few with his sand wedge from about eight feet, and he made eight out of ten! I explained this drill gave him low expectations and therefore reduced pressure. "Think how little effort you're putting into aiming the club," I said. Then we went back to the putter and his putts started dropping. Darren had regained his confidence. Once he got his putting back on track, it took a lot of pressure off his pitching and full swing. He went on to win the Open Championship that week with a score of 275, three strokes ahead of Dustin Johnson and Phil Mickelson. Darren Clarke had gone unconscious and became an instinctive putter again, and he was the "champion golfer of the year." You have to learn to get out of your own way and get back to being athletic with your putter and unconsciously reacting to your target—if you want to become the best putter you can be.

CHAPTER 11

Late Bloomers and Late Starters: Always Time to Chase a New Dream

How old would you be if you didn't know how old you was?

—Satchel Paige

When you look at three of the greatest athletes of the modern era—Tiger Woods, Michael Jordan, and Tom Brady—only one was destined to be dominant in his sport from an early age. Tiger was a child prodigy, he was shooting par at age five, and he was winning tournaments soon after. He continued to win early and often, capturing three US Junior Championships and three US Amateurs before winning the NCAA individual title at Stanford and then turning professional. He seemed a lock for greatness almost from the beginning because he combined his giftedness with passion and ambition. Now in his forties, he has amassed fifteen major championships and eighty-two tour victories—and counting.

Jordan got cut from his junior high school basketball team as a sophomore, then he started getting good his senior year in high school. Coach Dean Smith was criticized for taking a chance on Michael and offering him a scholarship at the University of North Carolina, where he became a star. While playing for UNC, he made the deciding basket in an NCAA Championship game. MJ said that lit his fire and helped him realize he could become great. And he dominated the NBA for more than ten years.

Then you have Brady. Unheralded in high school, he was barely decent enough to get to the University of Michigan, where he hardly got any field time the first two years. He improved enough in his last two seasons to catch the attention of the pro scouts, but even so, Brady was only the 199th pick in the NFL draft: *199th!* That year, six other quarterbacks were drafted before he was, not exactly something to cheer about. His first season with the New England Patriots was nothing to write home about either, the team finishing 5-11. He had to be patient, and he had to have faith that his day would come. It finally did, but it took a while. Things started to fall into place for Brady during the next season. It was a grueling year with five losses, but the Pats pulled it together in the playoffs and managed to make it to the Super Bowl. There, Brady didn't have his best game against the St. Louis Rams, but it was good enough. New England squeaked out a win, 20–17, on a 48-yard

How Old Are You?

As Satchel Paige also said, "Age is a question of mind over matter. If you don't mind, it doesn't matter." Here are some other thoughts about age:

- Are you so old that you value security over everything else?
- Have you lost the ability to be innocent enough and young enough to not know any better?
- When was the last time you were young enough to have the fun and joy of a young child?
- Are you thinking and acting old at a premature age?

field goal on the final play of the game, and the victory launched an amazing career for Brady. Over the next eighteen years he went on to play in nine Super Bowls and collected a total of six Super Bowl rings. This chapter is about the Tom Bradys of the world, and other late bloomers. It's also about late starters—those who came to golf later in life.

Whether you are a late bloomer or a late starter, you would do well to keep Tom Brady's story in mind, as well as Michael Jordan's. Many readers of this book have not had the time or the resources or the opportunities to concentrate on golf before but want to now. Maybe the opportunity was not there early in your life. Maybe you didn't even know about golf as a kid. Maybe you knew about it but didn't like it. Maybe you didn't care for an individual sport—you preferred team sports. Or maybe you thought golf was boring, or not physical enough, or took too much time. Perhaps as an adult you started liking golf but had to make a living, pursue a career, become financially secure. Or maybe you played a lot of golf at a young age, gave it up to go to college and raise a family, and now you're ready to seriously get back into it. Maybe you loved golf all along but didn't have the best instruction or weren't practicing enough or were practicing the wrong things or lacked confidence in your ability. Whatever the reason, you have finally decided to spend more time seeing how good you can get because down deep you always had that desire to find out.

Take heart in knowing that you're not alone. It is possible to get really good at golf, or to reach whatever goals you've set in the game, at just about any age—if you put your mind and soul into it. Others certainly have done it. One of the great qualities about golf is it's not necessarily a young person's game. It's truly a game for all ages. Numerous golfers took a long time to get to the top. Some got a late start. Some went in nonproductive directions before they figured it out. Some focused on other priorities before deciding that they wanted to concentrate on becoming the best golfer they could be.

Many late starters have been quite successful in other endeavors they have pursued. They think they should automatically be good at golf because of their success in business or in life. It is not necessarily so. I have to remind people of how much energy and time—usually many years—they put into their career to attain the success they had. Many of the principles that help them be successful in other aspects of their life apply. Taking on a quest in golf is going to require great patience, persistence, and belief in your potential, even if other people wonder why you care so much about improving your golf game and constantly ask why you're putting so much time and energy into it.

Interestingly, precocious youngsters have other issues to deal with. They must handle out-of-control expectations because the game came easily and early to them and they find themselves winning quite regularly. From an early age, they constantly have adults praising them and telling them they have unlimited potential. As nice as this sounds, it can put extra pressure on them and lead to problems. But these are very different issues from the issues that late bloomers or late starters face.

Whether you are getting into golf later in life or just haven't had much success in the game so far, you are ready to make a major commitment now. Much like in other aspects of your life or career, it's a good idea to be a visionary and to see yourself improving and succeeding in your goal or your dream. I encourage you to make a plan and create a culture inside your head and in your relationships with those people who can help you in your quest. You need to sustain a commitment. Ideally, your practice will be efficient, and you'll put the most time and energy into the parts of your game that are the most important to lowering your score. For many people, that means concentrating on your short game, spending quality time rehearsing all the short shots on and around the green—pitches, chips, bunker shots, and, of course, putting.

The legendary player Paul Runyan understood the importance of mastering all the shots around the green and even wrote a book about it. One of his two PGA Championship victories came at the expense of Sam Snead, who was outdriving him by fifty yards in their thirty-six-hole match-play final in 1938. Runyan got the ball up and down from everywhere and defeated Snead, 8 & 7, for the title. I worked with Paul for years in the Golf Digest Schools. He had big dreams well into his nineties and amazingly played in the Par-3 Tournament at the Masters at age ninety-one! Like Runyan, you can create your own dreams and aspirations that others don't even know are there. Runyan's quest was to break the all-time record of beating one's age by the most strokes. From age seventy on, he chased that every day. He probably broke his age by as many as fifteen strokes multiple times in casual play. It's amazing how many people get excited about shooting their age. In Runyan's case, he did it so many times he lost count. "Ninety-nine percent of the time, I beat my age," he once said when he was in his nineties. "I can still have a terrible game and beat my age."

According to *Golf Digest*, Bob Charles holds the record for most strokes under one's age in a tournament. He shot a 66 at age seventy-six in a European senior tour event. The record for a nontour event is held by John Powell. At age eighty-six, Powell shot a 64—twenty-two strokes better than his age—in a Southern California PGA section senior tournament in 2017. Walter Morgan is the youngest player on record to shoot his age in a tournament. He fired a 60 at age sixty-one on the Champions Tour.

These feats all point to how you can always keep aspiring to lofty goals in golf—as well as new goals in the game. Some amateurs only got really good in senior amateur golf. Some players on the PGA Tour and LPGA took years—even decades—to finally succeed. Others had virtually no career on the regular tour, but thrived on the Champions Tour. Look at Tom Lehman, who struggled for years as a professional on the mini-tours before finally turning himself into a major player, winning the British Open, becoming a Ryder Cup captain, and then winning tournaments on the Champions Tour. Or Bernhard Langer, who was certainly good in his twenties and thirties (he won two Masters and was tough as nails in the Ryder Cup), but truly excelled after age fifty, winning more than forty events on the Champions Tour. Or Calvin Peete, the pro with a diamond in his tooth. Before Peete discovered golf, he was selling jewelry and other items out of the trunk of his car to migrant workers. He first picked up a golf club at age twenty-three, turned pro at twenty-eight, joined the PGA Tour at thirty-two, and won the 1985 Tournament Players Championship at forty-two. He ended up leading the tour's Driving Accuracy statistical category ten straight years.

If You Weren't a Child Prodigy

So many of the truly successful players we see at the top of the leaderboards today were child prodigies. Not just Tiger Woods or Lexi Thompson or Rory McIlroy, but Justin Thomas, Matt Wolff, Lydia Ko, Collin Morikawa, to name a few. It's much easier to have big dreams when you're a prodigy and everyone is telling you that you can do anything you put your mind to. But if you are a late bloomer or late starter, that's okay, too. If you can't get yourself to have some long-term, grandiose dream, and if you're going to just set short-term goals, you have to constantly reset them as you knock them off. The advantage you have is, in general, you're the only one expecting much of yourself. You don't have the pressure that the precocious kid has, and so anything you do, any kind of positive outcome, is considered great.

Mark Wilson and Adam Long, both of whom I've worked with, have had to endure either the PGA Tour Qualifying School several times or long stints on the Web.com and Korn Ferry Tours before meeting with success and winning PGA Tour events. Similarly, Dana Quigley had an unremarkable professional career, never winning on the PGA Tour, then blossomed much later in life on the Champions Tour, where he has won eleven times. Dicky Pride was not a standout at the University of Alabama, and though plagued by injuries and health issues, he played on both the PGA Tour and Web.com Tour for twenty-five years. In 2015, he won the last regular-season Web.com Tour event, his first professional victory in twenty-one years, jumping from fortieth to fifth on the money list, and earned a PGA Tour card for the next season. Mike Goodes, an amateur in North Carolina who didn't even play on the golf team when attending UNC, turned pro at age forty-nine, qualified for the Champions Tour, and has retained his card every year since 2007.

Then there is the unlikely road to golfing greatness of Larry Nelson. The three-time major champion and Ryder Cup star didn't even touch a golf club until he was twenty-one years of age. He was busy playing other sports in high school, going to college, and serving in the Vietnam War. He started playing golf after returning to his native Georgia from Vietnam. While finishing up classes at Kennesaw State, he fell in love with the game—a golf course was right next to campus. He never played junior golf, never played collegiate golf, never even played much amateur tournament golf. He taught himself by reading Ben Hogan's *Five Lessons* book, worked on his game with a fellow veteran and golf instructor, and practiced long and hard every day. Though he broke 70 within nine months, he didn't qualify for the PGA Tour until he was twenty-seven years old. (By comparison, Tiger had won thirty-one PGA Tour events and seven majors at age twenty-seven.) But Nelson became one of the game's most feared competitors, winning the 1981 and '87

PGA Championships and the 1983 US Open. In his first two Ryder Cups, in 1979 and 1981, he compiled an unprecedented 9-0-0 record. Later, on the Champions Tour, he won nineteen times. Nelson didn't care that others had a massive head start in the game. He set his sights high, dreamed big, and believed in his destiny, then did what was necessary to make it happen.

Tom Kite and Pat Bradley, likewise, blossomed somewhat later in life. Kite, who won nineteen times on the PGA Tour, came into his own in his early thirties. He became the tour's Player of the Year in 1989 at age forty and won his only major, the 1992 US Open, at age forty-two, after he had been on tour twenty years. Upon turning fifty, he became a force on the Champions Tour, winning ten times. Bradley bloomed in her thirties, going seven lean years after turning professional before claiming her first major title, the 1981 US Women's Open. She won three of the four women's majors in 1986, her breakout year, at age thirty-five, and won a total of seven majors. When she won her thirtieth tour event and so was inducted into the LPGA Hall of Fame (her lifelong dream), she started looking for a new dream and became captain of the Solheim Cup. Ben Hogan struggled for seven years on tour before he won his first tournament and didn't win a major for another eight years, seventeen years after turning pro. What's also interesting is that Kite was getting beaten by Ben Crenshaw as a junior, Bradley was losing a lot to Nancy Lopez on tour, and Hogan even as a kid was losing most of the time to Byron Nelson in caddie tournaments.

Another late starter was Allen Doyle, who didn't even turn professional until age forty-six, the same age Jack Nicklaus was when he won his *final* major championship, his sixth Masters. Doyle played sporadically on the Nike Tour for two years, then started competing on the PGA Tour at age forty-eight, making about half his cuts. But when he turned fifty, he joined the senior tour and came into his own, winning an amazing $13 million in prize money over the next several years, including back-to-back US Senior Opens.

There's also the amateur Bill Shean Jr., whom I've worked with. After dedicating himself to running an insurance agency and putting all of his time and energy into the business and his family, he decided to see how good he could get at golf and devoted about ten years to that dream. He won two US Senior Amateur Championships (1998 and 2000) and a British Senior Amateur (1999). When he was ready, he really made a commitment to becoming as good as he could be at the game. Joel Hirsch, like Shean from the Chicago area, was a similar example. After playing college golf at the University of Houston and University of Illinois, Hirsch decided to focus on creating an insurance business because he felt he wasn't good enough to compete on tour. Twenty years later, with his business solidly in shape, he started concentrating on competitive amateur golf. He qualified for the Western Open for the fourth time, at age fifty-eight, played in nine US Amateurs, and won two British Senior Amateurs, among numerous other tournaments.

I'd also consider another Hall of Famer, Betsy King, a late bloomer. After she joined the LPGA Tour in 1977, it took her seven years and a lot of patience to win her first tournament, the 1984 Women's Kemper Open. She won two more times that season and was named the LPGA Player of the Year. Her game had finally fallen into place. She recounts that she and her teacher, Ed Oldfield, made some significant swing changes— getting her clubface less shut at the top and swinging less from the inside and more down the line. They also made her putting stroke longer and more fluid. But there was a mental discovery as well: "I thought that to win I had to play perfect golf for four days in a row," she said. "I realized that you can make mistakes and still win. It's how you handle your mistakes. That took a lot of pressure off me." In the next five years King won twenty LPGA tournaments, more tournament wins than any other golfer in the world, man or woman, during that period. After that first win in 1984, she won at least once in each of the next ten years, and six times in 1989, when she was the leading money winner.

As you can see, some athletes and a few golfers who made it big were prodigies from an early age, but many struggled and got really good later in life. It's never too late and it doesn't matter when you start. It's all about where you go with what you've got, and finding a way. These players all found a way. To do that you have to go on a mission. But it's important to have fun on your mission, finding out what you can do with your talent at a game that you love.

You have to understand that there are expectations you put on yourself and those that other people put on you. You should care only about *your* goals and *your* expectations that you've set for yourself. If you're a late bloomer, you have to believe you could beat some child prodigy who maybe beat you for years in an earlier life. But now you've improved your skills, and part of it is realizing and telling yourself, "Hey, when they play me, they have unbelievable pressure because they think they're supposed to beat me, and they're going to look bad if they don't." Sure, they might have had some successful experiences against you and others, but they also have pressure now. Remind yourself that the pressure is on them, not on you. It also goes back to remembering to be process-oriented and not outcome-oriented. Make sure you're living your own expectations and not the expectations of others.

Sometimes, those becoming late starters think they are being selfish. They feel guilty about putting themselves and their dreams ahead of other priorities. But that's counterproductive. I'm not asking you to give up your life and relationships. I just want you to commit to some time each day to see how good you can get at golf with part of your life. At some point you have to ask yourself, "Is it worth it to me?" and "What price am I willing to pay to see how good I can get?" If you truly want to do this and pursue your ultimate dream, then you need to have a laser focus or a tunnel vision, so that you know what your priorities are and how much time and energy you are going to put into it. During that time, nothing gets in the way or distracts you from your mission. It might seem self-centered and egocentric, but not making you and your dream number one in your life might also be a shame, a lost opportunity. You have to constantly feed your faith that you're going to achieve your quest.

If you've never played competitive golf or if you haven't played a lot of competitive golf in a while and you start competing again, the strong tendency is to feel uncomfortable. The other players you are grouped with or who are warming up next to you before the round have been doing this all along. Some players who are not used to that environment will tell me they play worse when they are paired with better players, perhaps the defending champion or a bigger-name player. But others tell me they play better with better players. My answer is that both groups are too involved with their pairings. No matter who is in your group, or what the situation is, tell yourself, "I've got my own little way of doing stuff, and I'm playing my game, and I'm executing my plan no matter what, and I will get in this state of mind and mood regardless of the situation."

You might be riding in a cart with someone who never says a word, or someone who is a chatterbox, or someone who just wants to talk about his own game or what he did on a certain hole the day before. You need to do everything possible to let nothing bother you once the round begins until it ends. Stay unflappable and be disciplined about keeping in the moment. Concentrate on *your* game plan, *your* pre-shot routine, and what *you* normally do before, during, and after each shot. Get lost in your game and your own world that you create in your head. This is what you own and can control.

In competition, you need to eliminate distractions, get rid of the limits, and be fearless if you want to find out what you can do. You need to keep putting yourself in competitive

---

What Freddie Jacobson Learned from Bernhard Langer

After his first win on tour, the Swedish player Freddie Jacobson said, "I had to take a look at myself and wonder why one man in my group had the right stuff—Bernhard Langer—while another did not—me. I just had to realize that I wanted it too much. I could see how relaxed and how much into the process he was. He was probably one of the best at that. [Distractions are] going to pop up, like after ten or twelve holes some guy driving by in a golf cart saying, 'Well done, buddy.' You are leading and you could get stuck in those words, but I took it like 'Okay, I went through this a couple of weeks ago. Let's get back to just hitting good shots and see where it ends up.' All the wins I have had, I have been in a nice quiet place, where I feel very happy, where I'm at peace with my game."

situations—entering and playing in competitive events—until you get used to it. And if you don't have butterflies before and during a round, it might just mean it's not important enough to you. Jack Nicklaus told me that he couldn't play his best unless he was nervous. He *wanted* to be nervous. Later in life, if he didn't play his best, it was because he didn't feel nervous anymore. Bill Russell, even after winning numerous NBA championships, would still often throw up before important games. He actually welcomed that. It indicated the upcoming game meant something to him. I'm not saying you need to throw up before a competitive round, but my point is that even the best players feel their hands are shaking when they're putting during a serious competition. They learn to deal with it and even welcome it.

If you are a late bloomer or a late starter, it might take many months—even years—of losses before your game falls into place and it is your turn to shine and dominate. A number of late bloomers and late starters have used others who don't believe in their mission to motivate them to prove the so-called experts, the naysayers, wrong. Another way to go is to build a support network that believes in you and your ability and what you are trying to accomplish. That could include a golf instructor, a physical trainer, a nutritionist, a mental coach, a spouse, or a family member. You need to be able to talk to them honestly about what your goals and aspirations are and have them give you direct feedback so you can keep improving and striving for your dreams.

You might start thinking that to excel at golf later in life is nothing short of miraculous. Well, I want you to live your life as if everything were a miracle or as if nothing were a miracle. Just because you haven't found success—yet—there is no reason why it can't still happen, if you *believe* it can happen. Just ask Gary Burkhead, the former vice chairman of Fidelity Investments. I started working with Gary when he was fifty-nine. He knew that to enjoy retirement and be motivated he needed a goal, a challenge. He wanted a reason for getting up every morning and having a purpose.

The mission he chose was to see how good he could get at golf. He set an extremely high goal for himself, to go from being an 18-handicapper to playing in the US Senior Open. He developed an effortless and simple routine. He committed to being unflappable and process oriented. He then committed to spending several hours, six days a week, on his short game, both on and off the course. He tried a few different instructors until he settled on one and came to closure on his swing. They kept it simple, unconscious, and flowing. If anything, Gary plays better in competition, and I have never seen him get upset on the golf course. Over time, he saw massive improvement in his golf game. Eventually he missed qualifying for the Senior Open by a couple of shots, but he got down to a 2 handicap and got good enough to shoot even par in a senior mini-tour event competing with pro golfers, an incredible accomplishment. He won various tournaments and club championships in south Florida and on Cape Cod. At seventy-nine, he is still loving the challenge.

CHAPTER 12

Winning Big—
Maintaining a Healthy
Perspective on Golf and Life

The future belongs to those who believe in the
beauty of their dreams.

—Eleanor Roosevelt

T his book is about chasing your biggest dreams and going
for greatness, always striving to make your next shot your
best shot. But there is a lot more to life than winning on the
golf course, and a lot of people eventually realize this. This is
what we can learn from some of the most successful winners
in sports—and in life. Starting when I was seventeen years
old, I had an opportunity to work with physically and mentally challenged kids at a swimming program for five straight
summers. These special needs children I was coaching were
categorized as "mild," "moderate," and "severely challenged"

in their mental and physical issues. They were all living at the Brandon Training School in Brandon, Vermont, near where I grew up.

After graduating from Castleton University, I accepted a full-time teaching position at Brandon Training School and also started coaching basketball at the high school I attended, Mount Saint Joseph Academy. While I was at Brandon Training School, some faculty members at the University of Connecticut came to evaluate my teaching and ended up offering me a scholarship to graduate school, where I earned a master's degree in special education. However, as a coach, I became deeply interested in sport performance, so I completed another master's degree and a PhD in sport psychology. While studying at UCONN, I also coached lacrosse there and basketball at E. O. Smith High School, so I gained a lot of experience coaching all types of kids and athletes.

But those special needs students I worked with during those summers made the biggest impression on me. I learned a lot about attitude while teaching those kids. They might have ninety-nine out of one hundred things going wrong in their life, but they would spend all day excitedly talking about the one good thing they were experiencing. It was a marvelous ability. It taught me to keep things in perspective, and I'll never forget the lessons I learned from them. It taught me about the power of perception and of focusing on what you have, rather than what you don't have. Some of these young people were facing incredible odds against succeeding not only in sports, but in life. Yet, they had the most positive attitudes, and they didn't care what other people thought of them. They were focused on succeeding, no matter what it took. These kids placed no limits on themselves and chose to be happy and passionate about whatever they were doing.

Why are some people born lucky, with natural physical and mental talents, and others are not? I don't know the answer. But I do know that true champions learn that a strong mind, a pursuit of their goals and dreams, and a dedication to hard work is much more important than athletic ability. This same approach can also greatly enhance your enjoyment of life beyond sports.

Jordan Spieth gained a similar outlook because of his special needs sister. Brooks Koepka talks of putting his golf into perspective after visiting a children's hospital near his home in Florida. Gary Woodland has become good friends with Amy Bockerstette, an inspirational young golfer who has Down syndrome, after the two connected in an emotional video at the 2018 TPC that went viral. "You've seen the people that have been impacted by this, by the video and her attitude, her energy, her love," Woodland said. "I keep saying it, it's so contagious and the world needs a lot more of it. And especially with everything that's going on in the world right now, we need a lot more Amy in it." Woodland reconnected with Bockerstette the following year and credited her with inspiring him to win the US Open at Pebble Beach. He also donated $25,000 to the I Got This Foundation, named for her declaration when she got the ball up and down in that TPC video.

"I got this!"

—Amy Bockerstette

Jack Nicklaus, heavily influenced by his wife, Barbara, devotes much of his time to raising money for their charity, the Nicklaus Children's Health Care Foundation, supporting veterans' programs, and advising other up-and-coming players. But even during his prime, Jack's family was his first priority—he focused on his marriage, his five kids, then later his grandkids. He usually played in no more than fifteen tournaments a year, hence the PGA Tour's Jack Nicklaus Rule, requiring players to enter a minimum of fifteen events to keep their tour card. Jack rarely missed one of his kids' games, sometimes even flying home during a tournament to see one of his sons—Jackie, Gary, Steve, or Michael—or daughter, Nan, play in one of their games, then flying back to the tournament the next morning in time to tee off.

Gary Player was similar. Despite flying all over the world to play in tournaments and exhibitions, he and his wife, Vivienne, focused on raising the best family possible—four daughters and two sons and lots of grandkids. No one is more dedicated to as many nongolf activities and to bettering humanity than Player. He had such an influence on Nicklaus that Jack and

Barbara named their fourth child Gary. It all reminds me that even though we tend to worship some of sports' biggest stars because of what they do or have done on the course, on the court, on the field, or in the ring, it's the lessons they teach us in other aspects of their life that can put us on the path to winning big, to being the best we can be, not only at the game of golf but outside it as well.

I believe that Nicklaus's approach to life helped him be a winner in golf because his attitude reduced the magnitude of the outcome in his mind. In effect, he minimized the pressure by saying that his nongolf activities were more important. He listed ten of his thoughts on winning in his book *Playing Lessons*, which he wrote with his longtime collaborator, Ken Bowden. I have touched on a number of these topics in earlier chapters, and they are as relevant today as they were when Jack wrote them:

1. Learn the fundamentals of a good swing and putting stroke and stick to them through thick and thin.
2. Practice more than you play . . . especially the short game.
3. Play yourself and the course . . . never the person or the field.
4. Play to a plan on every hole, and be totally realistic about your capabilities and the prevailing conditions.
5. Keep your cool . . . *accept* that golf was never meant to be a 100 percent fair game and that you are human and therefore fallible.

6. Don't compound your errors or unlucky breaks . . . be conservative in your recovery strategy.

7. Live in the present . . . think about and play only one shot at a time.

8. Play your hardest from the first tee . . . golf is an eighteen-hole game, not a one-shot or one-hole contest.

9. Never hit a "quit" shot, even in practice . . . keep on trying whatever happens.

10. Whether you win or lose, enjoy the experience of competing.

Kobe Bryant was another great example of someone who looked well beyond the game he excelled at. Before the NBA superstar tragically went down in that helicopter at age forty-one with his thirteen-year-old daughter, Gianna, he was living

The Perspective of George Burns

The vaudeville star and legendary comedian George Burns once told a bunch of kids on the Disney Channel, "You either love what you do or you learn to love what you do. I don't see where there's another option." He lived to be one hundred years old.

every day for the betterment of young basketball players and athletes and devoting much of his time to his Mamba Foundation to help underserved kids realize their dreams in sports. He certainly wasn't perfect in his early career and life, which has been well documented, but he became a true role model and was admired by his teammates, his opponents, his peers, and his family. He had ten rules he followed that can be applied to all sports. The NFL champion Philadelphia Eagles taped a copy of Kobe's rules on a wall in their locker room. These can certainly apply to golfers who want to be as good as they can be:

1. Get better every single day.
2. Prove them wrong.
3. Work on your weaknesses.
4. Execute what you practiced.
5. Learn from greatness.
6. Learn from both wins and losses.
7. Practice mindfulness.
8. Be ambitious.
9. Believe in your team.
10. Learn storytelling.

These are all things that you can do to become the best you can be at golf—and in life. Most are points that I have discussed earlier in this book. However, the last point is especially important. To be the best golfer you can be, you need to create your own story, your own reality, your own dreams, imagining them as successful as possible, then doing everything you can to fulfill them. That's how great storytelling can help *you* to reach *your* goals. It takes an undying belief in yourself and your abilities, but you can do it if you put your mind to it.

Lydia Ko is continually writing her own story, literally. The Korean-born golfer was a child prodigy growing up in New Zealand and the youngest person—male or female—to become No. 1 in the world, at age seventeen. She was also the youngest player, at age fifteen, to win an LPGA tournament, and the youngest, at age eighteen, to win an LPGA major. Then she lost her way for a while, but through a positive attitude and strong work ethic she made the journey back to the highest levels of the game. At age twenty-three, she wrote a fictional letter to herself as if she were still fifteen years old, which was published by Golf Channel's Randall Mell in 2020. We can all learn from her matter-of-fact, positive approach to keep the game in perspective:

"Golf is hard," she wrote. "That is why so many fans come out to see it being played well. They understand the hours on the range that it takes to build a solid, repeatable golf swing. They understand the sweat and frustration that goes into thousands of bunker shots. They appreciate the dedication it takes to make 100 six-footers before dinner. And they appreciate the nerve required to hit shots under pressure.

"There is good news. Just as quickly as the game can slip away, with hard work and self-belief it can come back. And

What Kobe Bryant Learned from
Michael Jackson (and Others)

Kobe Bryant often told a story that when he first went to
the Lakers, he decided he wanted to excel in the game
as much as possible. So he got in touch with the singer/
dancer Michael Jackson because he wanted to pick his
brain about success. Jackson told him he had to study
greatness, and that he, Jackson, got a lot of his ideas for
singing and dancing from Gene Kelly's scenes in the movie
Singin' in the Rain, and Jackson said he tried to take it to
a whole other level. From that, Kobe decided to visit with
Hakeem Olajuwon to study his pivot moves. Kobe spoke
with Michael Jordan to learn anything MJ might tell him. And
Kobe went to Jerry West, who told him that he loved that
Kobe believed in himself, but to stay humble if he wanted
to be great. Olajuwon later said that a lot of people think
Kobe Bryant was arrogant and egotistical, but he said all
he could tell you is that Kobe was with him for seven days,
all day each day, and no one could pay more attention to
learning about how to get better than Kobe did. So the
moral of this story is, to fulfill your greatest potential don't
hesitate to seek out advice from the very best, and work
at it as hard as you can.

when it does, you will be stronger and wiser for having traveled the rough road to get there.

"A few more things you should know: Your golf swing may come and go, but your family and friends, the people who care about you, will love you no matter what you shoot. Trophies are symbols of what you've accomplished in the past. Your family and friends represent who and what you can be in the future. Their hugs, their presence, their laughter, is life's greatest victory.

"Others will criticize you and will question those around you, assuming you are being manipulated or led. Those criticisms and accusations will wound you—knives thrown at those close to you always cut deeper than those you field yourself—but they also make you stronger and more appreciative of the people who stand by your side. Just as you are responsible for the shots you hit in competition and the scores you post on your card, you are also responsible for the decisions you make that got you there. The advice of others is important. But the decisions are yours. Own them. Be you. And be happy. Do that, and everything else is going to be fine."

Other words of wisdom from coaches in other sports can help to guide you in golf. My dad, Guido "Guy" Rotella, a wise man who lived to be one hundred, was a huge fan of John Wooden, the legendary UCLA basketball coach who won ten National Championships in twelve years. My dad's favorite John Wooden line was "Never lie, never cheat, never steal, don't whine, don't complain, and don't make excuses." Wooden said he got that from his father, who imparted those words to his four sons. Wooden also espoused the following advice that golfers would be smart to adhere to:

- Be enthusiastic about your work.
- Don't get angry when people test you.
- To get cooperation, you must give cooperation.
- Don't be afraid to fail.
- Pay attention to the little things.
- Be loyal to yourself and to your organization.
- Remember that success is not defined by victories.

Wooden also said, "All winners and losers in life are totally and completely self-determined, but only the winners are willing to admit it." He never scouted another team because he believed that if his players executed their stuff, they could beat anyone. Another legendary coach, Vince Lombardi, often said the same thing, and contrary to public opinion, he would agree with Wooden's contention that success is not defined by victories. Lombardi was famously quoted as saying, "Winning isn't everything, it's the only thing." But my cousin Sal Somma, who was a highly successful football coach at New Dorp High School in Staten Island, New York, told me that when they did coaching clinics together, Lombardi, who was coaching at St. Cecilia High School in Englewood, New Jersey, always told him that he borrowed that line from a football coach at Vanderbilt University named Red Sanders. Lombardi said, "I

We know what we are, but not what we may be.

—William Shakespeare (also PGA Tour
player Matt Wallace's tattoo)

don't know what *he* meant by it, but what *I* meant is making the *commitment* to winning is everything. I meant putting the *effort* into winning. I meant having *that* be your purpose." Lombardi also said, "I wasn't talking about the final score or the outcome of the game. Many times when I was coaching, we would lose and I felt we gave it our all and played the way we were capable of playing. I'd be the first guy in the locker room to congratulate the players and pat them on the back and tell them how proud I was of them. There were other games that we won on the scoreboard and I felt like we failed to play to our ability level, and I was the first one to kick 'em in the butt." A lot of times when you play great to win, people start thinking that winning is all that matters. That's not the case, though it's certainly preferable. But I want you to go out on the golf course and see how great you can play, and play without fear, play with confidence, and if it doesn't add up that day, so be it. You can live with yourself. You have no regrets. You gave it a chance.

To win, however, you must not think of winning while pursuing it. You must think of the process and stay in the moment, rather than thinking of the outcome. It's like Mexican great Lorena Ochoa's approach to golf when she was on tour—and to life in general—which she described for *Golf Digest* in the summer of 2020: "Every day, I did an analysis of everything: the way I think, the way I walk, the way I communicate with my caddie, the way he answers, the way he looks at me, the way we walk, the rhythm—so many little details that I think are very important."

I admire Lorena for having the courage to walk away from competitive golf when she did because she was following her heart, not trying to please someone else's expectations for her career or her life. Like Bobby Jones in 1930, Lorena retired from competition at age twenty-eight while at the top of the game, and she says she has never regretted it. She had just been inducted into the LPGA Hall of Fame after twenty-seven tour victories, including two majors, and winning the Rolex Player of the Year title four years in a row. She decided to move on and focus on raising a family in Mexico (she now has three kids) and devoting much of her time to her foundation (a school for underprivileged children based in Guadalajara), which she says is what she is most proud of.

"The better I played, the more I was able to give back, to start a foundation and help many, many kids," she said. "The foundation was always my motivation when I was playing. Today, we've had more than five thousand kids already pass through the school. We've impacted so many lives. God gave me the opportunity to play good golf to help others. That's something special, and I'm going to continue to do that."

Finally, when I think about the best lessons that pertain to golf and life, I am constantly reminded of my student and friend Gary Burkhead, an incredibly gifted and motivated person whose story is detailed in chapter 11, "Late Bloomers and Late Starters." Gary, at age fifty-nine, decided he needed a new challenge. He made it his goal to go from an 18 handicap to a 2, and he achieved it by working unbelievably hard and doing it systematically, working with a golf professional, a fitness trainer, a nutritionist, and me, practicing six to eight hours a day, six days

These Words Hung on Arnold Palmer's Office Wall

Whether You Think You
Can or You Can't
You're Probably Right

If you think you are beaten, you are;
If you think that you dare not, you don't;
If you'd like to win, but you think you can't, it's almost
    certain you won't.
If you think you'll lose, you've lost;
For out in the world you'll find success begins with a
    fellow's will.

It's all in the state of mind.

If you think you are outclassed, you are;

You've got to think high to rise;

You've got to be sure of yourself before

You can ever win a prize.

Life's battles don't always go

To the stronger or faster man;

But sooner or later the man who wins

Is the man who thinks he can.

a week, often spending several hours just on his short game. He met that goal and has won several senior club championships in Florida and on Cape Cod. But in doing so, he never forgot the principles that made him highly successful in business. He wrote a short book about his life and career called *A Wonderful Life*. He published it only for his children and grandchildren, and it documents the principles that have guided him throughout not only his career in the insurance and financial business until he retired as vice chairman of Fidelity Investments, but also through his life in general, coming from humble beginnings in Little Rock, Arkansas, graduating from Columbia and Harvard, and making it big. At the end of the book, he devotes some pages to a number of life lessons: "Approaching the World; Presenting Yourself; Leading a Meaningful Life."

Some of the main principles include:

- Set high goals and make a plan to achieve them.
- Conquer your fear of failure.
- Use eyes, touch, and space to build relationships.
- There is no substitute for hard work.
- Avoid drugs, alcohol, and tobacco.
- Show respect for all people.
- Find positive ways to relieve stress.
- Practice good posture.
- Do the right thing, always.

But there is much more. Under the heading "Always Give Your Best," Gary wrote something that pertains to the theme of this book, making your next shot your best shot:

It's important to give your best, even when you're not working on important projects. Over time, giving your best will become your habit. You'll feel satisfied that you have never shortchanged yourself. Moreover, people around you will come to rely on you. In that sense, giving your best helps you build great relationships with people. Some of my friends say they could be better at golf if they took lessons or practiced more often. Really, they don't commit because they fear that they would not be great golfers even if they gave their best. Don't let that sort of fear get in the way of giving your best. . . . While I'd like to be as good as Tiger Woods or Brooks Koepka or Rory McIlroy—the best golfers in the world today—I am not them. I'm satisfied knowing that I'm as good as I can be. Give your best always, and no matter how you perform, you too will feel this kind of satisfaction.

How the NFL's DeMarcus Walker Excelled at FSU

When he played for Florida State (he now plays for the Denver Broncos), DeMarcus Walker told *USA Today* that he would push his body so far past its limits in the brutal Florida summer that he would throw up. He called these sessions Throw Up Mondays. (These were not Florida State workouts. He did them on his own.) He went from being an average player to the best defensive player on the team. He made sure he worked hard enough to throw up because he said he wanted to be the best. "I love perfecting my craft and getting better," he said. "I hate pain but I love pleasure. So the sacrifices I have to make to prevail, I don't mind doing [them]." This is a special mindset, wanting something so badly and having so much conviction that you voluntarily put up with that kind of pain. It says a lot about Walker's work ethic and his driving self-belief to be the best.

Gary's advice about life in general are words we can all aspire to and live by. Here are some of my other favorites:

Measure Your Self-Worth Properly: Of course, we care what people think of us and how they view our success. But other people's perceptions and expectations should not determine how you view and value yourself. *Think about what's important to you, what you would like to accomplish, and what is meaningful to you. Examine that periodically.* If you do that, you can assess properly how your life is progressing—and whether you're living up to your own expectations.

Show Humility: Humility wears much better than arrogance over time. Let your achievements speak for themselves. Give credit to others for what they accomplish. If you do this rather than tell people how great you are, you'll end up with respect and admiration from many people. Social media interferes with humility. Facebook, Instagram, Snapchat, Twitter, and other social platforms encourage us to call attention to ourselves. Remember, people who are humble about what they've achieved in life end up getting the most respect.

Make Integrity Your Compass: Integrity and trustworthiness are the most valuable aspects of character. If you compromise your integrity, people will never forget it. They will change the way they think about you. Follow through with what you commit to do. And always tell the truth. If you treat integrity and trustworthiness as your most precious assets, you will be well rewarded.

Eat Well and Exercise: Nutrition plays a major role in how you feel, how much stamina you have, and how you perform. I urge you to study nutrition. [My wife] Dawn and I have a nutritionist who helps us address our own various health conditions. It's easy to rely on fast food. It's best to avoid it altogether. I ran two marathons. And I ran daily until my knees would no longer allow it. Now, three times a week, I do resistance and cardiovascular work with a trainer. It really makes a difference. Respect your body, and take care of your health every day.

Know That Family Is Most Important of All: As I look back, I regret that I didn't spend much time with my family during my working years. When I faced prostate cancer, I rethought my priorities. I realized that family is more important than anything else. The family provides the framework and setting for love, support, teaching values, giving help, celebrating successes, coping with disappointments, friendship, and so much more. The commitment of family members to each other enriches all their lives.

Finally, I believe that this advice from Gary might be the best anyone could offer or practice:

Do What You Love and You Will Love What You Do: It's a great idea to build your life plan around your strengths and your interests. You'll find your life fulfilling. You'll work harder. And you'll get value back from your hard work. Do what you love, and you will do well.

I promise you that if you are loving what you do, you will definitely be happier. And who doesn't want to be happy?

It's like what Muhammad Ali, perhaps the greatest boxer of all time, said at age thirty-five when contemplating his retirement from the ring: "He [God] doesn't praise me because I beat Joe Frazier or some other boxer. He wants to know how we help each other. I believe we're going to be judged. Going into real estate, going into business, that won't get me to heaven. He wants to know how do we treat each other, how do we help each other, so I'm going to dedicate my life to using my name and popularity to helping charities, helping people, uniting people." Ali followed through on this pledge, lending his name and time

You have to expect great things of yourself before you can do them.

—Michael Jordan

to many charities and causes around the world, most notably the Make-a-Wish Foundation and the Special Olympics. "I've always wanted to be more than just a boxer," Ali said. "More than just the three-time heavyweight champion. I wanted to use my fame, and this face that everyone knows so well, to help uplift and inspire people around the world."

As Gary Burkhead would say, Ali did the right thing.

Tom Kite, whom I've worked with since the 1980s, is another person who always does the right thing. When we first met, he said, "You know, I love the way you talk about dreams, instead of goals."

"Why is that?" I asked.

"Well," Tom said, "to me a goal is something when I was a kid that some adult told me I should do, and if I did it, I was going to be a good little boy and get a pat on the back, and if I failed to do it, I was going to be a bad little boy and get a spanking." And he looked at me, and said, "But dreams are all mine. They're my ideas of my life. As long as on the day I retire I can look in the mirror with a big grin on my face and say I got to get up every day and chase my dreams, I'm going to die a happy man. It's not going to matter how many trophies I collect or how much money I make, that's all I want out of life."

As Kite will attest, in all my work with athletes over the years, I have learned that dreams are just ideas in people's heads. Everyone is just a person born to a mother in a small town, a big city, this country, or some other country, and you get to make up your own ideas for your own life. Because it's *yours*, be sure to choose wisely, and be sure to believe in *your* ideas and go after them with passion. Remember, sports in life are just games, and we do them a lot better if we *play* at them, and just remember to not take life too seriously. None of us get out of here alive anyway.

Epilogue

The optimist sees opportunity behind every difficulty.

—Winston Churchill

I have spent my life encouraging, discovering, and chasing human potential. I have taught many players that you must have a vision of what you will become and where you want to go, and you must be able to reject the naysayers who disagree, and you must be strong enough to get past the many setbacks along the way. I have taught many players that anything might seem impossible until someone does it. Suddenly, it is doable. And sometimes you might have to be the first person to do it. You *might* have to be the one who leads the way.

As many of the golfers and other athletes I have worked with might tell you, it's pretty obvious that I love teaching people how to believe in themselves. Only when you truly believe in yourself can you make your next shot your best shot. That supreme confidence in your ability to get the job done is your ultimate goal, and I get my greatest satisfaction when my students understand what is possible and that the word *impossible* does not exist. I love teaching players that it is okay to believe, and to believe in yourself more than anyone else believes in you. I love teaching people what it means to be committed and to be a True Believer. I love teaching people what it means to let go of anxiety and play fearlessly, what it means "to get out of your own way," and that *good* is the enemy of *great*.

I love teaching people to not feel guilty about being successful after they have put hundreds of days and thousands of hours into reaching for that success. But I also love teaching them that even after a huge victory you must love getting up the next morning and starting all over. I love teaching people that it's possible to have fun working hard at seeing how good you can get. I love teaching people that it is important to learn from their bad days, then to let them go. I love teaching people that you have to have the courage to find a way that works for you and to be willing to do it *your* way, even if it's quite different from someone else's way.

I love teaching people that you get results by being process oriented, not by thinking about results while you're playing.

I strive to get the best out of every player I work with. In my mind, I believe there's a way to get that player to a whole new level. Many times I see talent in people that they might not see in themselves. I find that when I'm working with players, it's as if time stands still and doesn't seem to matter. I usually forget to take a lunch break or take time to eat at all until my wife reminds me that I need to give my students some nourishment. I love mesmerizing people about what they are capable of doing.

Early in my career as a sport psychologist, I learned that Vince Lombardi would bring the entire Green Bay Packers team over to his house for a backyard cookout with their families. He didn't call it team building, but he knew that's what it was. He felt that was extremely important, maybe more important than coaching on the field. I was also influenced by Thomas Jefferson's design of the University of Virginia and the Lawn, which was the original grounds at the university, so that all the students lived on the ground floor and the faculty lived upstairs. Jefferson believed that the most important learning took place outside the classroom. Lombardi and Jefferson were the two people who had the most influence on my having the players I work with come and stay at my guesthouse at my home in Virginia.

I decided it would be great to have many of the players I work with come and stay with me for two days. I found it to be the best approach to making significant progress with my clients—with no distractions—and I still do it today. It's a tremendous way for the players to build trust, gain confidence, learn how to stay in the moment, and appreciate and believe in their talents and, ultimately, in their dreams.

I've always been intrigued by how many people are scared to admit that they have a lot of talent, because it means that if they don't perform well, then it must be their fault—so it's safer to pretend they don't have talent. I see this amazing phenomenon a lot, and I try hard to get them past that.

I have spent my life teaching golfers to be confident and believe in themselves and their skills, but I also want this confidence to be based on abilities that are primarily attained through sustained and diligent effort. Confidence is not easily acquired. It seldom comes without a lot of effort, at least not in this wonderful game of golf. It must be earned, challenged, and tested. Through this, confidence has more character and lasts longer. I have always gotten the greatest satisfaction from helping players who have put in the time and energy and honed their skills but who still struggle to trust themselves and their skills in competition. They deserve to believe in themselves and in these skills, and it is most rewarding when they learn to do so.

Working hard and having skills does not guarantee confidence, but it's a great place to start. For most of the best players in golf, their confidence is justified as a result of skill development. Methodical, consistent preparation typically results in confidence that is long-lasting and rock-solid. Confidence that is not developed and learned this way is usually fleeting and short-lived. Be sure that *your* confidence is based on an investment of time and energy, and don't feel bad if it has taken you a while to develop both your skills and your confidence. It's the way it is for most players—even most of the very best.

I try to be great at what I do every day I do it. It takes a lot out of me. Usually, I'm exhausted at the end of the day. But by the next morning I can't wait to start all over again! Every day when I look at a student, I try to treat that person as if he or she will be the next "great one" that I get to work with. I never know when I'm starting with a new student who is going to be the next star. But I always remember to appreciate that they trusted in me enough to come and spend two or three days (and many phone calls) with me in helping them develop their game. A side of me finds it hard to believe that I've gotten to do what I've been able to do for a lifetime. I feel blessed and fully appreciate the opportunity to live my dreams of coaching so many highly motivated and talented players.

I know exactly what I want when I'm working with someone, and I know exactly what I'm looking for. Sometimes it becomes obvious that a player will just not trust and come with me. But when I can get through to someone and get the person to believe and commit to having a great attitude, it is amazing what comes out of those players. What I see consistently is players who are able to get into a great state of mind and catch it when they are half an inch away, to become consistently great players.

There is always joy and satisfaction in helping players reach their dreams, winning big events, and leading a happy and healthy life. But there is a different joy in helping those who are child prodigies, who everyone else thought should and would win, versus helping late bloomers who no one else thought would ever win. These individuals bring different issues, and they present different needs and different challenges. One of my greatest pleasures in life is helping them reach their dreams— which includes long-term success with both their golf games and their personal lives. If you set your goals as high as possible, follow the principles I've laid out in this book, and always strive to make your next shot your best shot, I am confident you will find a path to your ultimate success with your own game.

My life is my work, my play, my friends, and my family—and my belief in a God. I treat my clients like family. That is my joy. I always have time and energy for my family and my clients. I have been blessed with great parents; loving aunts and uncles and cousins; a fabulous wife, Darlene, who is the love of my life, together with my daughter, Casey; her husband, Michael; and eight grandchildren. I have been a lucky boy and have lived a joyful life doing what I love, living my dreams.

Acknowledgments

As in my previous books, I am blessed with a lot of people to thank. I have had an incredible opportunity to coach and to learn from many of the greatest golfers and teachers of this era, and most of them are mentioned in the text of this book. I want to thank them all. I would also like to acknowledge the following, to whom I am grateful: Michael Baruzzini, for his editorial assistance; my agent, Rafe Sagalyn, for his guidance and support; to the folks at Acushnet Company and Titleist, who have always been there for me; as well as to Summit Brands; and to the editors of *Golf Digest* for their support of my work over the last forty years, as well as to Stephanie Frerich and Emily Simonson at Simon & Schuster for seeing this book through to its completion.

About the Authors

Dr. Bob Rotella is the most recognized and preeminent sport psychologist in the world. He has written nine books on the mental side of sport, including the bestselling *Golf Is Not a Game of Perfect*. His eight other books, including *Putting Out of Your Mind* and *How Champions Think in Sports and in Life*, are loved by golfers and nongolfers alike.

Dr. Rotella was the director of the Sport Psychology Department at the University of Virginia for twenty years, and he has worked with athletes in many sports, from basketball to baseball to tennis to lacrosse to swimming to even horse jumping—and, yes, to golf. Within the game of golf, he has worked with all kinds of players, from rank beginners to such major champions as Padraig Harrington, Tom Kite, and Pat Bradley. There is hardly a player on the PGA or LPGA or Champions Tour who doesn't know "Doc," as they affectionately call him.

Since 1984 Rotella has coached the winners of seventy-four major championships in men's, women's, and senior professional golf. In 2011, he helped Darren Clarke win the British Open and Keegan Bradley win the PGA Championship. Rotella has also helped singers and businesspeople. Anyone whose work or play involves mental challenges can benefit from his proven wisdom.

There's nothing mysterious about Rotella's approach to performance. The bedrock concepts of his philosophy—free will, commitment, persistence, and confidence—are things he learned as a boy and high school athlete in Rutland, Vermont. They're lessons he reinforced by observing famous coaches such as Vince Lombardi, Red Auerbach, John Wooden, Dean Smith, and John Calipari. They are principles that apply not just to sports, but to many endeavors. One of Rotella's gifts is his ability to figure out how each student will best understand and adopt these principles.

Rotella's clients have also included many corporations, such as Merrill Lynch, General Electric, and Time Warner. He taught in the Golf Digest VIP Schools for many years, where he worked closely with such renowned teachers as Bob Toski, Jim Flick, Peter Kostis, and Davis Love Jr., and he has written countless articles for the magazine as a professional adviser. Rotella lives near Charlottesville, Virginia, with his wife, Darlene. They have one daughter, Casey, and several grandchildren.

❖

Roger Schiffman began his career at *Golf Digest* in 1979 and was the managing editor from 1984 to 2013. He has written more than three hundred articles on various aspects of the game. He continues to write articles for the magazine as a contributing editor and has worked mostly with legendary player Jack Nicklaus and Hall of Fame teachers Jim Flick, Jim McLean, Rick Smith, Chuck Cook, and Martin Hall. Prior to joining the *Golf Digest* staff, Schiffman was associate editor for the US Golf Association's *Golf Journal* and the US Tennis Association's *Tennis USA Magazine*.

Schiffman has written five books on golf: *Golf Basics* (1985); *How to Win the Three Games of Golf*, with 2004 PGA Teacher of the Year Hank Johnson (1993); *Perfectly Balanced Golf*, with 1996 PGA Teacher of the Year Chuck Cook (1997); *A Golden Eighteen*, a four-hundred-page coffee-table book celebrating eighteen of Jack Nicklaus's signature golf courses throughout the country (2014); and *A History of Quaker Ridge*, celebrating the club's one hundredth anniversary (2016).

Schiffman is also the founder and director of Fairways for Freedom, which conducts trips to Ireland, Scotland, England, Nova Scotia, and US destinations for combat-injured veterans.

A graduate of the University of Missouri, Schiffman holds a BA in journalism. A 2-handicap golfer, he splits his time among Cape Cod, Jupiter in Florida, and northwest Ireland with his wife, Dr. Patricia Donnelly, a sport psychotherapist. Their daughter, Kate, is a licensed mental health counselor in Boston.